SURVIVING
BETRAYAL

SURVIVING
BETRAYAL

Counseling an Adulterous Marriage

Donald R. Harvey

Baker Books

A Division of Baker Book House Co
Grand Rapids, Michigan 49516

© 1995 by Donald R. Harvey

Published by Baker Books
a division of Baker Book House Company
P.O. Box 6287, Grand Rapids, MI 49516-6287

Printed in the United States of America

Library of Congress Cataloging-in-Publication Data

Harvey, Donald R. (Donald Reid).
    Surviving betrayal: counseling an adulterous marriage / Donald R. Harvey.
      p. cm.
    ISBN 0-8010-4396-4
    1. Marriage counseling. 2. Adultery. 3. Pastoral counseling.
    I. Title.
BV4012.27.H375 1994
259′.1—dc20   94-29017

To the many couples with whom I counsel.

Though crises and chaos go hand in hand,
there is nothing beyond the redemption of God.
Though it is he and not counselors
who brings healing and restoration to hurting lives,
I am honored to be used in the process.

Contents

Quick-Scans

Introduction

Surviving Betrayal deals with marital restoration—restoration in relationships that have been brought to a crisis by infidelity. Though marriage counseling is a profession for which I have been trained, much of this book is the result of my experience. I have observed that the act of marital betrayal is excruciatingly painful. There is little that will create any more functional havoc and emotional intensity for a marriage than unfaithfulness. It is my strong belief, however, that even the crisis of infidelity can be survived and a betrayed marriage can be completely healed and restored. Restoration of this magnitude does not come easily. Great effort is involved, and it necessitates the active commitment of both partners to a restoration process and a therapist who can artfully lead them through the progressive steps of healing.

There must be healing within the relationship. My goal in writing *Surviving Betrayal* is to identify for those who counsel the whys and hows to obtaining this end. In it, I both espouse a philosophy regarding the healthy restoration of an adulterous marriage and provide a specific model for intervention. Philosophically, infidelity needs to be viewed from a first-things-first perspective. *You must first deal with the affair before you can proceed to the more important work of restoring the marriage.* Affairs are usually symptomatic of a marriage that was lacking in one way or another. (This does not justify the act of betrayal. It merely aids in our understanding.) There were issues in the marriage that allowed the relationship to become susceptible to infidelity. Though these issues are historical in nature and existed long before the affair occurred, they are still present even though the affair has ended. In fact, they will continue to be an interference for the marriage until they are appropriately identified, addressed, and resolved. The natural tendency of many counselors is to begin the restoration process by addressing these issues. This temptation must be avoided. This is not the means by which healing comes to a relationship. Though your ultimate goal is to deal with these core marital issues, before you can successfully deal with the marriage, you must first resolve the affair.

The focus of *Surviving Betrayal* is on facing and resolving the affair—the act of betrayal. Once this is accomplished, the couple is ready to face the marriage. Resolving the affair requires that a couple accomplish several tasks. The progressive steps toward restoration are clearly identified in this book, as are the role and intervention strategies of a counselor. Part 1 describes the chaos of the initial presentation. The couple who first comes to your office has a relationship in complete disarray—both functionally and emotionally. In the midst of obvious relational confusion, however, the Lord can bring both order and peace. Part 2 presents a model for intervention and restoration. This is the plan of action. Based on the first-things-first philosophy, its goal is in resolving the affair and not necessarily dealing with the core relationship issues which have historically frustrated the marriage. The specific steps in resolving the affair are identified and explained. Part 3 describes the common interferences to resolving the affair. If life were ideal, this section would be unnecessary, but life is seldom ideal. Though a couple may want restoration, there are common attitudes that can stand in the way of reaching this goal. To continue the move toward healing, identification and resolution of any resistance to the restoration process must be accomplished. Part 4 brings closure to the book and allows for a transition to what is more traditionally viewed as marital therapy. If a couple has safely journeyed to this point in the restoration process, they are now ready to deal with the core marital issues. *Surviving Betrayal* is written in a nontraditional style. I have intentionally avoided much of the formality and technical jargon that often accompany a work written to professionals, and I have included several case illustrations and stories. *Surviving Betrayal* actually represents a middle-of-the-road approach. At one end of a continuum would be found most books aimed at instructing in the art of therapy. On the opposite end of the continuum would be works like *The Family Crucible*, Whitaker and Napier's classic depiction of family therapy through the novel-like chronicling of the experiences of one family. My aim is to provide a clear, concise, cohesive, readable, and easily applied intervention strategy.

To further aid in practical application, Quick-Scans are strategically placed throughout the book. These easy reference guides contain specific intervention steps in a summarized format. Rather than having to skim several pages to refresh your memory of the specific nuances of a particular stage in the treatment process, you need only to locate the appropriate page in the list found immediately following the contents.

To avoid the awkwardness of the endless use of "he or she," I have often chosen to use the male pronoun for the offending spouse. However, adultery requires the participation of both a man and a woman—it is not an exclusively male or female problem. The principles and applications in this book can be applied to any couple, whether the offending spouse is a man or a woman.

Surviving Betrayal has been a joy to write. I hope that this book, and especially the model for intervention, will be helpful for you in your work with people in adulterous relationships.

Part 1

Order and Chaos

1

The Taylors

Linda and Carl Taylor sat in my office during our first counseling session. Projecting an image of conservative middle-class America, they were pleasant, nicely dressed, well educated, deeply religious, and strongly committed to their church. As we talked the differences in their dispositions were noticeable. Linda was expressive and warm; Carl was gracious but extremely retiring. Cordial glances were being exchanged, as well as cordial words. There was no bickering, no harshness.

It was a pretty picture, but only an illusion. I knew the idyllic presentation was false because I already knew more about the Taylors than they had shared in our brief conversation. There had been an affair. One of them had betrayed the marriage. And whenever there is betrayal the consequence is disruption.

Linda and Carl had been referred to me by a colleague. With their permission he had shared some of their history. They had both been raised in stable, middle-class, Christian homes and had started dating in high school. Linda's first recollections were glowing.

Carl was quiet and shy when I met him. Not much has changed on that account. He seemed so reserved. He didn't smile or laugh, and he didn't talk much either. I had to do most of the talking, but that has never been difficult for me.

I knew at that first meeting that there was something special about Carl. I cared for him right from the start. Part of it might have been that he seemed so lonely and I just wanted to make him feel better—to help. I've always had a compassionate streak. But mostly, there was something different about Carl—something that I hadn't sensed in any of the other boys that I had dated.

Carl impressed me as being reliable. I felt that I could trust him with anything—no matter what it was. I knew that I could count on him to be honest and genuine with me. And I grew to love him for that.

Carl's response surprised me. He was elaborate and almost poetic, expressing his recollections with real emotion. This seemed out of character.

I remember our first meeting. Linda approached me in the hall between classes. It was like walking out of the shadows on a cool day into a stream of sunlight.

I was kind of a loner back then and kept pretty much to myself. I hadn't dated very often up to this point. I just didn't feel comfortable approaching girls. Then Linda popped into my life. She was so cheerful. I had a hard time knowing what to say at first. But that didn't seem to make much difference. Things were just always easy between us.

I was surprised, but happy. There was no discomfort when I was with her. She added a dimension to my life that I had never before experienced. I had never felt loved like that before.

I really liked the way I felt when we were together. Linda was so alive; being with her seemed to give me life. It was all so natural. Linda just stepped in and filled a void—this big *hole in my life. We were good for each other right from the start.*

I couldn't help but wonder where and when things began to go wrong for them. Both Linda and Carl had given such favorable reports of their beginning. What had precipitated their deterioration? Why the infidelity?

In addition to knowing about their respective families and how and when they met, I also knew that Linda and Carl married while in college, that both of them graduated, and upon graduation, both entered careers. Carl chose to utilize his talents in business and finance by working with a religious organization. He had worked there for nearly twenty years and had reached a high position of responsibility. Though the work was personally fulfilling, the financial rewards were not commensurate with other things that Carl could have chosen to pursue.

Linda chose a career with a Christian publishing company. She also found this challenging and rewarding. Working in Christian publishing was more than a job for Linda. There was a real sense of ministry that accompanied her investment of time—a satisfaction of being used of God.

I also knew that Linda and Carl worked for several years before they had children. Life was uncomplicated during those early years. Then came the three children. In addition to the normal adjustments that are required in parents' lifestyles when children enter a family, the Taylors' situation was complicated by the fact that one of their children had a chronic illness necessitating quite a bit of attention. After several years of attempting to balance two full-time careers and the needs of a growing family, the decision was reached for Linda to quit her full-time job and stay at home with the children.

Life had been hard for the Taylors, at least during the past several years. Greater responsibilities at work had necessitated longer hours for Carl. Yet with all of his effort, finances always seemed to be tight. Linda continued her work at home on a part-time basis. Though she was free to spend more time with her family, and the flexibility worked well around the fluctuating health of her children, this arrangement meant obvious limitations to her career and a decreased income. It seemed as though there were always more needs than there were solutions. When energy was spent in bringing order to their careers and finances, home became chaotic. When energy was redirected toward bringing order into their home, finances became chaotic. The payoff for order in one area was chaos in another. No matter what they did, life was difficult.

Life had been difficult for the Taylors, but is difficulty in life all that unusual? Though names, places, and events vary from couple to couple, many marriages could echo Linda and Carl's complaints. Life can be difficult. Interruptions can be frustrating. Setbacks can be disappointing. Unreached goals can be demoralizing. Difficulties seem to bond some couples closer together. They work together, pull together, and share each other's pain and joy together. To use a scriptural analogy, the trials which they encounter burn off the dross of the marriage, and what emerges is a refined and precious metal—a core of strong commitment to one another (see 1 Peter 1:7). For other couples, external pressures seem to drive wedges between spouses. Stress pushes them apart. My theory is that the wedges are already there. Stress merely accentuates the problem. It is like holding a piece of broken pottery up to a light. The light merely illuminates the cracks; it does not create them.

Had difficulties in life precipitated problems for the Taylors? It was possible that external circumstances had started the deterioration of their marriage. Yet the stresses alone, at least those of which I was aware, would not have led me to suspect that one of them would have an affair. Everything still appeared too stable, too moral, too right for that to happen.

So here we were, meeting together for the first time. I already knew so much about Linda and Carl, yet there were still unanswered questions. It wasn't that what I already knew was unimportant. To the contrary, I needed to know all of this information. Still, these pieces of information were only happenings—benchmarks in time. As such, these events acted as no more than a skeleton. They were important, providing a structure, but they did not provide much meaning. It would be Linda's and Carl's perceptions and misperceptions of these happenings, their reactions to these events, and their consequential emotions and feelings toward each other that would place flesh on this skeleton and enable me to make some sense out of what had happened.

As we sat in my office, I could not help but think that Linda and Carl presented an amiable image. Even their history was unremarkable. It was easy to think: "Who would have guessed it?" "Who would have thought that there would have been an affair?" Yet I realized that as we got into the meanings of their relationship, the true significance of these happenings in their marriage would be disclosed. More than merely witnessing events, we then would understand the hows and whys of Carl's infidelity. We just needed to delve a little deeper.

2
The Emergence of Chaos

It did not take much to move us from an atmosphere of superficial pleasantries to one of emotional intensity. I merely asked, "Why are we here?" Conversation stopped. Smiles disappeared. All body movement ceased. It was as if I had pressed the pause button on my VCR. What had been a very animated scene was instantly reduced to a still shot. After a few moments, I attempted to aid in their dilemma by stating that I was already aware of much of their situation, but I really wanted to hear each spouse's perspective on why we were meeting together, what had happened in their marriage, and where we were going.

It was clear that Linda and Carl had only been visiting the abode of pleasantries. Their true residence was that of marital estrangement. The tension that filled my office was suffocating. The first indication that the frozen posture was thawing came with movement in their eyes. Linda and Carl began to look at each other—each searching for an indication that the other would begin the conversation. It did not come. We continued to wait. Linda motioned to Carl with a nod of her head. Though no words were spoken, she was clearly asking Carl to start the interchange. Carl remained motionless. Finally, Carl uttered the first words. "Why don't you begin, Linda?"

Linda was reluctant to take the lead. I didn't know whether she found the subject uncomfortable, feared Carl's response, or did not want to be cast in the role of an attacker. But she probably realized that Carl could outwait her. Being more concerned with resolution than winning a power struggle, Linda succumbed.

For the past two years, Carl has been having an affair with a woman at work. I had no clue. I knew Carl hadn't been himself lately. I even thought he might be a little depressed. But I thought it was related to work. He had been putting in a lot of hours, and I knew he wasn't happy with some changes in the organization. I had no idea he was unhappy with our marriage. Carl never said a word to me about it.

About six months ago, I began getting telephone calls suggesting that something might be going on. I couldn't believe it and totally defended Carl. When I mentioned the calls to Carl, he just said, "they're crazy." Even at church, a few close friends asked me if anything was wrong. Again, I totally supported Carl and acted appalled that anyone would even think that something was the matter.

I was such a fool! My illusion of a stable marriage came crashing in on a Sunday morning. Carl said he wasn't feeling well and thought he'd just stay home and rest. I took the children and went to Sunday school. We returned after church to an empty house. Carl was gone. There was no note—no message of any kind. Some of his personal items were missing. But that was all.

I was in shock. What could have happened? I was so confused. I called some close friends, and they came over. We waited and wondered together. Finally, I called Sherry's husband. She was the woman who the concerned callers kept talking about. Sherry was also missing. My heart sank. That was when I fell apart.

That was in June. I didn't hear from Carl for three weeks! Not a word. He just walked out. He abandoned me—and he abandoned his children. We were left alone to contend with life, to deal with finances, to explain to friends and family, to wrestle with the whys and what ifs. It was a disaster.

By now, Linda's bubbly disposition had been replaced with tension and tears. She was sitting on the edge of her chair tightly gripping the armrests. Carl, on the other hand, had sunk as far back in his chair as he could possibly go. Linda paused for a few moments to see if Carl had anything to say at this juncture. There was no response. Carl's silence came as no surprise to me or to Linda. She continued.

Do you know what makes me maddest right now? I was finally starting to come to grips with my life. I was so torn up at the start. If it hadn't been for my children—having to stay strong for their sake—I probably would have cracked up.
It took several months, but I was finally beginning to pull out of the downward spiral. I didn't like what had happened—and I still loved Carl—but I was getting to the place where I could accept it. I knew I was going to survive. Then Carl dropped back into my life. I had no warning. He reappeared as abruptly as he had departed. All of a sudden all of my emotional progress went flying out the window.

Linda finally released her grip and collapsed back into her chair. She was done. Though she had been directing her words toward me, she was really speaking to Carl. Now she awaited his response. Carl continued to be silent and expressionless. His foot began to twitch nervously as he realized all eyes were on him. In a nearly inaudible tone, Carl finally said, "I don't know what to say." Not willing to let it go at that, I suggested that he simply tell me *his* story. "What's your perspective on all of this?" There was another pause. Then slowly, Carl began to speak.

It's like Linda said. I had been having an affair with Sherry for two years. It didn't start out that way. We were just friends. She was unhappy about things and so was I. One thing led to another. Sherry was just so easy to talk to.

I haven't been happy with our marriage for years. I began questioning whether things could ever be any better for Linda and me. We were so different. I doubted whether what I thought or wanted would count for anything anyway. What was the use of even trying?

Work was a disaster. Home was a disaster. The only good thing in my life was Sherry. I decided to shuck it all and be happy! So I left.

I know what I did was wrong, but I felt as though I had no other choice. I was so miserable. I had to survive. It felt so good to be with Sherry.

After a few months, the reality of what I had done began to hit me. I knew I had to come back. I knew I had to face my responsibilities. I couldn't abandon my kids. So I called Linda, Sherry called her husband, and we both came home.

Throughout most of Carl's account, his tone was hushed—almost sheepish. His words were calculated and deliberate. Occasionally he interspersed an otherwise expressionless performance with a smirk or grin that seemed out of place. After his initial response, Carl made some flippant comments: "I guess I messed up big-time." "I did the wrong thing." This could have been an attempt to lighten the heavy mood, but I believed there was more to his comments than that. I wasn't as concerned with the words as I was with the attitude.

Linda was easier to read than Carl. Though she showed some confusion, primarily she was intensely angry. Her anger had a singular focus: the pain of the betrayal. This pain was easy to understand. A terrible thing had happened in her life. Our society waters down the reality of what really occurred by using cute phrases like "an affair," "a lover's tryst," or "an extramarital relationship." I prefer to use the term *betrayal,* because it captures more of the essence of the pain. *Linda was betrayed!* She was deceived. She was rejected—cast off—for another person. And all of this hurt.

Linda was angry, and Carl was the focus of her anger. Once we got past the pretense of our introduction, it became very clear where Linda stood. She hid nothing, held back nothing.

Reading Carl presented a greater challenge. He seemed confused. He wondered how Sherry would fit into all of this. (I suspected that Carl had some lingering emotions for Sherry.) There was the question of whether things could ever be different for Linda and him. Carl did show some guilt and embarrassment for his irresponsible behavior, and he seemed to be wondering what was the right thing for him to do. Finally, he also seemed angry. I was not sure whether his anger emanated from resentment or from an attitude of justification, but I was fairly certain of its presence.

Unlike Linda, Carl masked his thoughts and feelings. This had been his pattern. For years he had avoided conflict and potential hurt by keeping things to himself. When pressed—when silence was no longer acceptable—his predictable response was always, "I don't know."

For years Carl had successfully avoided dealing directly with Linda. But I believed that there was more than simple avoidance—there was also resistance. Being quiet, tossing out humorous quips, making flippant responses, all of these maneuvers lessened the significance of an issue that Linda found to be important. This was Carl's indirect way of expressing his anger. He was a guerrilla fighter. He would not openly face Linda, but he could harass and sabotage her while remaining safely camouflaged. With this kind of history, getting Carl to honestly and openly deal with Linda would prove to be quite a challenge.

Accusations and Counteraccusations

We seemed to have broken the ice with their respective accounts of why they were at my office. Emotions were flowing freely as Linda and Carl diverged into a round of blaming. Linda resumed her position on the edge of her chair.

Linda: How could you do this to me? How could you? I've given my entire life to this marriage. I've loved you and have been totally committed to you. I didn't deserve this!

Carl: I know you didn't deserve this. I have done wrong. But our marriage wasn't perfect. It's not all my fault.

Linda: I didn't know you were dissatisfied. You never said anything to me about being unhappy. What was I supposed to do—read your mind? If you weren't happy, why didn't you say something? There was nothing that we couldn't have worked out. I deserved a chance!

Carl: I felt like you didn't pay attention to what I had to say. You listened to me, but you didn't really hear me. I told you I was concerned about finances, but it didn't seem to make a difference. I didn't see you go out and get a job. I told you I felt the kids were getting too much attention, but nothing changed. I told you I wanted our sex life to improve, but it didn't. So I finally told myself, "What's the use?"

Linda: We occasionally talked about these things, but I thought we came to agreements. I didn't know you were still unhappy. We both decided that I should quit my job and stay home with the children. I was working part-time, caring for the kids, and running the household. You were never there. What more could I have done?

I was less attentive after the children were born. That is true. Jason's medical problems only increased those demands. But that's reality, Carl. Things change when children come into the home. What did you expect me to do?

I had to spread myself around. I sure wasn't getting much help from you!

In addition to some of the historical marital issues, another area of contention centered around the events of the affair itself. Linda wanted to know facts. Carl was reluctant to share any.

Linda: Carl won't tell me anything about his relationship with Sherry. I have lots of questions. I don't know what happened, and I don't know what's going on now.

He says, "It happened and it's over. That's all you need to know." Well, I'm sorry, but I feel like I deserve more than that. There is a lot more that I need to know!

Carl: All Linda wants to do is to talk about the affair. I don't know what to say. It happened. I regret that it did, but I can't change that. (Turning to Linda.) It's over. What more do you need to know? Anything more will only cause you needless pain. Just accept reality!

The volleying continued for several minutes—point, then counterpoint. Linda and Carl were drawing the battle lines. Each was placing blame on the other—Linda, in her emphatic and emotionally expressive manner, and Carl, in his sullen and resistant posture. Linda seemed to be arguing that she was faithful, loyal, and responsible. She particularly resented Carl's failure to bring his complaints to her for resolution. She wasn't perfect, but neither could she read minds. She protested, "It's not my fault if Carl wasn't willing to deal with his dissatisfactions."

Carl sullenly clung to a position of being discounted. He claimed to have had little influence in the home. His opinions did not count, and Linda abandoned him and his needs for the needs of the children. From both perspectives, it was the other spouse who was at fault.

Linda and Carl were beginning to share meanings. The significance of the happenings in their marriage was being made known. Flesh was being placed on the skeleton of historical events, and what was coming forth was very enlightening.

Ambiguous Commitments

The more Linda and Carl presented their respective cases, the greater the question of commitment loomed in my mind. Were Linda and Carl committed to the marriage? Were they committed to the process of reconciliation? Were they willing to do what would be required of them to rebuild their relationship? It seemed as though they were asking the same questions, of themselves and of each other. Not surprisingly, it was easier to get a decisive answer to the question of commitment from Linda than it was from Carl.

I love Carl. I have always loved Carl. I didn't stop loving him just because he left me.

Carl says he wants to come back, so what choice do I have? I wouldn't look very Christian if I said no, would I? So I'm resigned to doing whatever it takes to make my marriage work.

My real question is with what Carl's willing to do. I know he's back, but why? And for how long? I still don't know if he's really committed or if he'll just leave again when things get tough. I don't think restoring our marriage is going to be easy. Is Carl going to stick around through the difficult times, or is he going to leave? I don't know, and he can't seem to say.

Carl began to bristle at Linda's remarks. After a few sighs and some squirming around in his seat, he offered his response.

This is part of my frustration in dealing with Linda. I don't know that I can say the exact words she wants to hear.

How do we define commitment? I can say that I'm back and that I have no plans to leave. I can also say that I want to work on our marriage. But is it a lack of commitment if I say I don't know that I'll be able to stay if things don't get better?

Multiple Problems

Though the affair was past tense, it had resulted in some additional present-tense problems. For example, the Taylors' financial standing was a wreck. Their family budget had been stretched for years. Carl's leaving home was equivalent to several months of unemployment. In fact, it was worse than simple unemployment. While away, Carl had attempted to establish a new business. His efforts were unsuccessful. The lack of income, coupled with the failed business venture, left Linda and Carl in a desperate financial situation.

Carl's leaving not only affected the Taylors' immediate financial status, it also had implications for their future earning capability. Carl had left his employer as abruptly as he had left his family. Though returning to his former position was out of the question, he was finding it difficult to find suitable employment of any kind. It was still too early to tell what long-range consequences Carl's behavior would have on his career, but things definitely were not looking good at the present.

Carl's decision to leave also had implications for Linda's employment. Discussing the pros and cons of full-time versus part-time employment, examining the trade-off of household chaos versus financial chaos, and rationally working these issues through to a point of resolution was a past luxury. Linda no longer had an option. She had to return to the workforce regardless of what that would mean for order at home. In all likelihood, there would now be chaos in both family and finances.

Carl's behavior had also resulted in significant social changes. Christian couples tend to have a narrow social base.

Activities are frequently church functions; friendships are largely church-related contacts. An event as detestable in the conservative community as a marital affair totally disrupts the social order. Carl's behavior had attached a stigma to the Taylors. Attending their church became uncomfortable. Relationships with friends were strained. Linda and Carl were both experiencing social alienation.

I feel as though I'm having to pay two times for Carl's irresponsible behavior. First was when he left. His departure devastated me. But now I'm paying for it in all the changes I'm being forced to make and with all the pressures I'm now forced to experience. We're about to go under financially; I've got to totally change my lifestyle; I'm going back to work; we've lost all of our friends; we've lost status and respect in our community; I can't even feel comfortable in my church. Where does it all end?

Linda accurately summed up their situation. There were financial pressures, lifestyle adjustments, and social repercussions, but these are only words until you realize the emotional impact which these have on the lives of people. Linda and Carl were finding the present tense as emotionally devastating as they had the past.

The Caricatures

After nearly an hour of conversation, a picture of the Taylors was beginning to come into focus. The relationship that they had developed, the meanings associated with their marital history, the whys and hows of the betrayal all began to make sense. But what was going to be the outcome of their marriage?

As I pondered that question, it became clear that their respective attitudes were not too encouraging. If words could be converted to pictures, I would have drawn two caricatures to represent the Taylors. One picture would have been of Linda, the martyr. The other would have been of Carl, the justified. Can you envision these caricatures in your mind?

Characteristic features of Linda's martyrdom were:

> "Carl hurt me!"
>
> "How could he treat me this way?"
>
> "He doesn't really appreciate my pain!"
>
> "I'm the one making all of the sacrifices!"
>
> "I'll be paying for the consequences of his behavior the rest of my life!"
>
> "I didn't deserve this!"

Most of these statements could have been accurate, but what struck me was the relational consequence of this attitude. Linda's martyrdom was keeping her emotionally distant from Carl.

Characteristic features of Carl's justified attitude were:

> "Yes, I did wrong, but it wasn't all my fault!"
>
> "Linda never gave me the attention I deserved!"
>
> "If she'd been a better wife to me, maybe I wouldn't have strayed."
>
> "I recognize my errancy, but I don't see me as dastardly as Linda does."
>
> "What's it going to take for her to just let this thing go?"

There was probably some truth in Carl's statements. Marital deterioration is usually a cooperative effort with contributions coming from two spouses. Rarely is it the product of one spouse alone. Linda could have been more attentive, but did her supposed lack in attention give Carl the right to have an affair? Though not stated directly, this seemed to be what Carl was implying. Carl's justified attitude was keeping him emotionally estranged from Linda.

Total Chaos

What a difference an hour makes. What began as a pleasant conversation rapidly deteriorated into one charged with emotional intensity. Before my eyes, this idyllic appearing couple transformed into two boxers, each throwing crushing verbal blows at an angry, yet tired and beleaguered, opponent.

At one time the Taylors had a stable relationship. They were lovers. But that was then and this was now. The word *stable* had been replaced. Our choices now were words like *unstable, chaotic, conflictual, belligerent,* and *dysfunctional.* Of one thing I was certain, Linda and Carl were no longer lovers.

Confusion was the order of the day. Every aspect of their lives was in chaos. Where do you begin to put back the pieces of a broken love? What will bring healing to a relationship devastated by betrayal? Is restoration hopeless? Is the task overwhelming? Are there just too many things with which to deal?

3

There Is Hope

The situation represented by the Taylors was desperate and chaotic, but it was by no means hopeless. The chaotic nature—the emotional disruption, the contextual turmoil, the personal confusion—only served to demonstrate the Taylors' normality. After all, betrayal is a horrible thing. Based on what had occurred, their situation was no worse and no better than most of the other cases of marital betrayal that I had witnessed. Nor will it be much different from what you will encounter. With the Taylors, as with the cases with which you will be confronted, there is the need for a little order.

On my wall is a calligraphy saying: "In the beginning God created order out of chaos. . . . He still does!" I believe that this is not only true for individuals and the personal chaos that can appear to be so overwhelming, but that it can have special meaning for marital relationships as well. My years as a Christian therapist have taught me that though not everything will be redeemed, there is nothing beyond redemption. We serve a redeeming God—a God who brings order to our lives and who desperately desires to bring restoration. We only need to do our part and be willing to let him do his.

Redemptive Joy

My daughter recently had to write an essay in an English class. Her assignment was to talk about her family and to relate what it was like to live in her home, including a description of the other family members. After the assignment was returned with a grade, Paige shared her insights with Jan and me. Part of her description of me was from a vocational perspective. "My dad is a clinical director, a teacher, a public speaker, and an author. But if you ask him what he does, he just says he's a 'marriage counselor.'"

My initial response was to chuckle at Paige's description. She seemed to have all the pieces of my fragmented life fairly identified. On a deeper level, however, she had articulated the difference between what I *do* and what I *am*. In my heart, I am a therapist. Marriage is my passion. I love to work with couples, somehow involving myself in the restoration process—being used of God to move a desperate situation from one of crisis and chaos to reconciliation and order. Being a clinical director, teacher, speaker, and author are merely expressions of what I do. I *direct* the activities of others as therapists, I *teach* others to be therapists, I *speak* about what it takes to have an enriched marriage or how to intervene in problematic relationships, and I *write* about my experiences. But at the core of these varied activities is what I am. At heart, I am a therapist. My compelling desire is to see restoration—to somehow be productively involved in redemption.

Meeting with Richard recently reminded me of why I do what I do. Though presenting a calm and collected composure, his inner life was anything but calm. Richard and Stacy were separated at her request. We were not yet meeting conjointly. Though Richard desired this and also longed to be back in the home, Stacy was not yet ready to consider actually working on the marriage. Stacy was in turmoil. She loved Richard, but she could no longer stand the relationship as it had been. Stacy wanted restoration but feared that the future would be no different than the past. She had lost hope.

In a session with Stacy I spoke to her about the redemptive power of God and the means whereby hope can be restored to a marriage. We discussed what would need to happen—what would be her responsibility and what would be Richard's. What Richard and Stacy needed to do was clear. Whether they would do it or not was uncertain. I knew if they were able to genuinely reconcile, there would be joy. I also knew that if they did not, there would be much sorrow. Richard's words haunted me. "I only hope Stacy will give me one last chance."

Seeing the pain expressed by both Richard and Stacy reminded me of why I am compelled to be a therapist. I do not enjoy seeing desperate situations. Nor do I enjoy being an observer of pain. But I do love being a party to redemption, and in genuine reconciliation, there is always joy—true joy.

Moving Apart and Coming Together

In an indirect manner, two very different biblical passages can be contrasted to underscore the theme of "joy in restoration." The first passage is commonly referred to as the story of the rich young ruler. It is found in each of the Synoptic Gospels (see Matt. 19:16–23; Mark 10:17–22; Luke 18:18–23). In it, a man of significance asked Jesus a question: "Good Master, what must I do to win eternal life?" (Mark 10:17; Luke 18:18). Jesus responded with a list of behavioral do's and don'ts, which the young man proudly claimed to have followed all his life. Jesus then asked him to sell all of his possessions, give to the poor, and come follow him.

The issue for Jesus was not wealth, but security. Jesus pointed out that his security was to be found only in his reliance upon the Savior. Jesus was not being arbitrary. Neither was he responding out of bitterness or contempt for the young man's wealth. He was responding compassionately to the young man's true need. Jesus' heart was "warmed to him," and in love, he sought to draw close to a young man—no less desperate than the rest of us—and to offer him the opportunity to also draw close to him. The young man's choice was clear, as was the consequence of this choice. He was not willing to give up the tangible control found in self-reliance nor the temporal security of wealth for an intangible and nontemporal faith, trust, and reliance upon the Savior. As Mark so aptly describes, the young man's countenance demonstrated his loss: "his face fell and he went away with a heavy heart" (Mark 10:22).

The countenance of the rich young man depicted in Luke's eighteenth chapter can be sharply contrasted with that of another man of means found only a few pages later. In the nineteenth chapter, we find the account of Zacchaeus. Though also a very rich man, Zacchaeus accepted Jesus' invitation, repented of his sins, and gave away his riches to make restitution.

See the difference? Can you sense the contrast in countenance? The rich young man responded to Jesus' invitation by walking away. Zacchaeus grabbed on tight—he embraced the Savior. The young man left filled with *sorrow;* Zacchaeus was consumed with *joy.* What do these two passages illustrate? Simply this: *There is no joy in moving apart—there is only joy in coming together.*

No one walks away—whether it be from spiritual light, a relationship with God, or a marriage—with happiness. Walking away is always accompanied by sorrow and oftentimes regret. There is no joy found in moving apart. Joy is only found in coming together—in accepting spiritual light, in embracing the arms of the Savior, and in restoring strained relationships. There is joy—true joy—in reconciliation.

The relationship aspect of the principle of walking away versus coming together is illustrated by another familiar passage found in the fifteenth chapter of Luke's Gospel, the story of the father and his prodigal son (see Luke 15:11–32). The son had grown tired of both life on the farm and the lifestyle of his father. He asked for and received his inheritance. His resources were quickly exhausted in riotous living. When the son finally came to his senses and decided to return to his home and genuinely seek his father's forgiveness, his father greeted him joyfully with great celebration.

Joy is found in coming together. Zacchaeus experienced joy, but the rich young ruler walked away and only experienced heartache. Sometimes joy is found in our coming *back* together. This reconciliation was experienced by the father and his prodigal son. Their reunion was truly joyful.

Reconciliation is God's grand spiritual design. It is a focal point in Scripture throughout both Old and New Testaments. It is why Jesus came—to provide a way whereby man could be reconciled to God. It is God's plan and goal. It should also be our way of life; we are to live reconciled lives. When there is reconciliation, whether it be between God and man or within a marriage, there is joy—true joy.

There Is Hope

Regardless of appearance, the one thought that must constantly be before us is this: There is hope. This hope is not based on what man can and cannot do. Nor is it based on your intervention skills. Though successful restoration may involve both, our hope is more accurately based on the redemptive nature of God. There is hope in Jesus. As therapists, our best work comes as a result of remembering an appropriate hierarchy:

God is *able* to redeem.
God *desires* restoration.
God can *use* the skills of those who are committed to him.

These first two statements attest to God's power and will. The last addresses our role and responsibility.

Situations may appear chaotic, and people may be desperate, but Jesus came to redeem otherwise hopeless situations and to transform desperation into joy. In the wake of marital betrayal, there is always relational chaos. But in the crisis precipitated by an affair, you can be the instrument used by God to bring order—to restore a marriage. Restoration rarely occurs spontaneously. Marriages in crisis need the aid of an experienced intervenor.

As a therapist, you are not responsible for what people do. You cannot control their actions, but you can influence their choices. You can listen, suggest, guide, and even probe if necessary, in an effort to aid a couple's attempt at genuine restoration. If successful, you can derive satisfaction from helping a couple move a marriage functionally from chaos to order and emotionally from sorrow to joy. "In the beginning, God created order out of chaos. . . . He still does"—even in disrupted marriages. And when he does, there is joy.

But what is to be done? What is the route? How do you aid a couple in moving from chaos to order? How do we move toward joy? Are there steps? Is there a process? What has to precede what? Are there some things that need to be done and others that need to be avoided?

When it comes to counseling with marital betrayal, there is a plan of action for the process of restoration that can be followed. The relationship needs to heal, but healing is a process— a process with identifiable steps. Your role as an intervenor will be greatly enhanced as you understand exactly what needs to happen. With a clearly identified plan of action, you will be equipped to aid in the redemption process. You too will participate in the joy.

4
A Plan of Action

Treatment begins with an accurate diagnosis. Knowing the role that each spouse has played in the development of the relationship, understanding how they have brought the marriage to a place of crisis, and knowing what they need to do for restoration are not only important aspects of treatment, they are essential. As a colleague once commented, however, knowing what people have done and knowing what they ought to do is not the end-all of treatment. Rather, *the real art of therapy is in getting people to do what they ought to do.*

Throughout the course of this book, there will be attempts to address what can be described as the "art of therapy." This is found in the suggestions for intervention. But counselors do not all practice the art in the same manner. Nor should they. Differences in philosophy and beliefs will influence what is done in therapy. Who a counselor is as a person will also influence what is done in therapy. Regardless of how you choose to intervene in the lives of a couple, however, there needs to be a plan of action. Though there is no guarantee that anything you do will necessarily bring restoration, having a clear plan of action will greatly enhance your potential for success.

Counseling is similar to taking a trip. Having a good road map always aids our arriving at the desired destination. In working with marital betrayal, the goal is restoration of the relationship, but the journey from crisis to healing can be long and eventful. Before we arrive at our destination, there are several stops that must be made. Though your practicing of the art may dictate a different negotiation of these stops, there is no place on our map that can be bypassed if we are to arrive safely at restoration.

The Ideal Trip

In an ideal trip, all of the travel plans occur without a hitch. The car doesn't break down. The hotel reservations are not lost or scheduled for the wrong day. All of the planned stops occur. It doesn't rain when you want to be outside. Everyone is pleasant to be around. And you don't run out of money.

Though not every trip goes as planned, some do. And when they do, we know what ought to be happening. That is what I'm describing in this section. When things transpire therapeutically in an ideal manner, what happens?

Beginning the Trip

Every trip has a beginning. The restoration of a marriage brought to crisis by the act of betrayal is no different. The journey toward restoration begins with the establishment of a therapeutic relationship. This is more than the mere formal agreement between clients and counselor to meet together. It is a relationship—a bonding and coming together based on honesty, trust, and caring. Without the establishment of this relationship, there will be no therapy.

During this early stage of the journey, several other activities will take place. Hypotheses regarding individual and marital health will be formulated as well as an assessment of the readiness of the couple to proceed. You will also prepare each spouse for the process upon which they are about to embark. As with most trips, we do not just simply begin. There is a plan.

An Early Stop

The order in which some of the stops on our journey are encountered will vary from couple to couple, but each must be dealt with. The affair will have to be remembered—faced and discussed. Actually, there will be little prompting for it to be remembered. It is ever present. The difficulty will be in getting the couple to face the affair and discuss it honestly. Facing it is a necessary step in placing it in the past.

Sometimes one spouse views discussing the affair as an attempt to "wallow in the mire." This is not the goal. You are not attempting to create any unnecessary pain or to inappropriately peer into an illicit occurrence. Rather, you are attempting to enable the couple to put the past behind them—to let it go. To do so will require a thorough immersion into the event. There will be a sharing of feelings, of the pain that the affair precipitated. There will be a disclosure of facts so that no questions go unanswered. With these two tasks accomplished, it is possible to place the affair in the past. There is no other way for this to occur.

Reconciling the Marriage

The restoration process makes a significant turn when the relationship is truly reconciled. As we will see, there is a sharp distinction between the acts of forgiveness and reconciliation. Forgiveness can occur without reconciliation, but reconciliation cannot occur without forgiveness. Reconciliation requires the cooperation of both spouses.

For a relationship to continue on the road to recovery, a genuine reconciliation must take place. Only through reconciliation can healing be brought to a marriage. And it is only through this healing that a couple acquires the desire to jointly pursue the remainder of the restoration journey.

Transition

After the affair has been faced and reconciliation achieved, the focus of treatment must move away from the act of betrayal to the relationship itself. This can be a difficult transition, but if the marriage is to be restored, it is a change that must occur. Most affairs are symptomatic of marriages that are troubled in some way. Certainly there are those adulterous relationships where a spouse has significant personality difficulties. These relationships are characterized by repetitive indiscretions. Whether for thrill, emotional neediness, or the bolstering of a sagging ego, the errant spouse is a sexual predator. Infidelity in these marriages is a pattern and not merely an incident. Though these types of relationships exist, they are not typical of the cases of betrayal you are likely to encounter.

The affairs with which you will deal will generally be *singular* in nature. Also, the betrayal will likely have been *unpremeditated*. Though decisions were made to pursue the indiscretion, the relationship was not begun with that intent. Finally, some degree of *marital dissatisfaction* was present. This dissatisfaction could have been obvious to both spouses, but it did not have to be. Marital failure can be a very subtle occurrence; some marriages just gradually and subtly drift apart.

Regardless of the form in which the failure crept into the marriage, the fact of the failure is clear. Couples who wish to bring their marriage to a point of restoration must be willing to (1) accept the reality that things were not great prior to the affair, (2) give up focusing primarily on the affair, and (3) begin dealing with the true changes required in their relationship. Without this transition, they will remain stuck.

None of this suggests the betrayal was warranted. Marital dissatisfaction does not justify betrayal. This is rather an attempt to bring understanding of how the betrayal could occur and of the work necessary for restoration. The characteristics that interfered with marital growth prior to the affair are still present and must be faced and resolved if the marriage is going to be restored to health.

What *Was* Still *Is*

Traditional therapy does not begin until you get to this place in the restoration process. The relational interferences in the marriage that allowed the relationship to move away from growth are still present. Now is the time to face them. Much of this book will be aimed at enabling a couple to reach the place where they can commence with traditional therapy. In essence, the couple must be ready to face their marriage and continue their journey toward restoration.

Detours

What has just been described is an ideal journey. Ideally, a therapeutic relationship will be established followed by scheduled stops involving facing the affair, reconciling the marriage, transitioning from focusing on the act of betrayal to recognizing the historical needs of the relationship, and finally addressing the interferences to marital growth. However, therapy, like travel, does not always go as planned. Sometimes we encounter detours. Some detours are natural and predictable—they can be anticipated in most couples. Others are more idiosyncratic—they may not appear at all, but if they do, they can be of substantial hindrance to our reaching the desired goal. Detours, whether natural or idiosyncratic, must be faced and resolved for restoration to occur.

Natural and Predictable Interferences

There are three areas of resistance that are so common that I suggest you expect to encounter them. They involve the attitude of the offender, the attitude of the offended, and the co-operative effort of both spouses.

1. "Let's just forget it happened."

Offenders typically do not want to talk about the affair. It is uncomfortable for them to do so. They would prefer to skip this part of the restoration process all together. Their preferences are commonly represented by statements similar to these:

"Let's just forget it happened."
"It's behind us now."
"God has forgiven me, and that's all that is necessary."
"Why bring something up that is in the past?"
"Talking about it will only cause needless pain."

Because of the personal discomfort associated with the betrayal, you can anticipate resistance from the offending spouse to dealing with the affair. Accordingly, you will need to be prepared to move the couple past this detour.

2. "Let's stay focused on how badly the affair hurt me."

As much as the offender desires to avoid dealing with the affair, the offended spouse wants to dwell no other place. He or she wants to talk about the pain, to describe the injustice, and to point out the contemptible indiscretion. Though some of this is necessary, the tendency is for an offended spouse to obsess over the affair.

"He really hurt me."
"How can I ever get over all of this pain?"
"I didn't deserve this!"
"She was despicable!"

Though the pain is real and the betrayal inexcusable, the marriage is not aided by maintaining a focus on the affair. This attitude must also be resolved.

3. "Let's not look at the marriage."

The two previous interferences represent a difference in opinion by the spouses. Whereas the offender did not want to discuss the affair, the offended spouse wanted to do nothing else but discuss it. With this third natural detour, however, husband and wife are typically in consort. Neither spouse may want to deal with the relationship—the historical marriage—the vehicle that got them to the point of crisis.

Dealing with a marriage requires work. Marriage is complex. There are contributions toward marital deterioration to be owned by both spouses. There will be the need for adaptation of behavior, expectations, or attitudes, and there may be the need for further reconciliation. Most couples are in favor of things being different in the relationship but opposed to making any changes personally. It's always the other spouse who needs to change. It is not difficult to understand the origin of this very predictable detour.

Idiosyncratic Interferences

Idiosyncratic interferences take on a less predictable nature. Some couples seem to be able to avoid them altogether. But when present, they represent far more formidable foes than the more natural detours just described.

The idiosyncratic interferences represent major blockages to the restoration process and can be deeply ingrained within a spouse. Getting a couple unstuck can be such a challenge as to warrant special attention in this book. The entire third section is devoted to this effort. The most commonly encountered blocks to restoration are represented by the following five attitudes.

1. "I can't get past the affair!"

This is the lone idiosyncratic interference inhabited by the offended spouse. It represents a tendency to obsess over the betrayal. Though a degree of this is predictable, an excessive amount exacerbates the problem.

2. *"I won't jump through hoops!"*

This blockage centers around personality characteristics and power struggles. The determination of what is reasonable to expect becomes crucial. In some instances, even knowing what is reasonable will have little to do with the solution. Resistance may be more strongly tied to personality issues.

3. *"I was wrong—but not really."*

Justification becomes the key focus of resistance with this attitude. The offender may grant lip service to having behaved poorly, but in his heart the affair was justified because of his spouse's failures in the marriage.

4. *"But I was hurt too!"*

Bitterness and resentment for past hurts underpin this form of resistance. It is differentiated from the attitude of justification by the fact that the offender does not feel his behavior was warranted by any deficiencies in his spouse. However, due to acts and events that occurred historically in the marriage, he still harbors bitterness toward his spouse. This resentment blocks his progress in the restoration process.

5. *"I can't let her go!"*

This interference to restoration is represented by a continued attachment to the illicit relationship. Though a physical relationship no longer exists, an emotional bond lingers.

Final Thoughts

Few trips are ideal. It is not likely that the journey you begin with a couple in search of restoration will be totally uneventful. Whether you encounter only the natural and predictable interferences or the more malignant resistances represented by the idiosyncratic attitudes, your role as a therapist will undoubtedly be challenging.

Still, there is at least a route to follow. *Surviving Betrayal* presents a plan of action. There are tasks that must be accomplished, steps that cannot be bypassed. Though you may choose to deal with these issues in your own style, you will find in this book a guide to marital restoration. May the Lord truly bless your efforts.

Quick-Scan 1

Steps to marital restoration

✓ Establish a therapeutic relationship.

✓ Face and discuss the betrayal.

✓ See that no questions go unanswered (complete disclosure).

✓ Give opportunity for genuine reconciliation.

✓ Resolve any blocks (resistance) to restoration.

✓ Effect a change in focus *from* the betrayal *to* the marital relationship.

✓ Deal with the core (historical) issues in the marriage.

Part 2

Resolving the Affair

5

Beginning the Process

Ideally, the first session will be a conjoint meeting involving both the offended spouse and the offender. There are times when an initial conjoint meeting just doesn't seem to work out. Sometimes individual sessions are requested and preferred by one or both spouses before determining whether further counseling is to be pursued. At other times, an appointment will be scheduled by a spouse whose partner is still reluctant to enter counseling. At still other times, you may meet with one spouse unbeknownst to the other. Regardless of the reason for meeting with only one spouse, it is to your advantage to then meet individually with the other spouse before proceeding with the first conjoint session.

Do not expect to bring any significant change to the relationship during this first conjoint session. Direct intervention is not the intent of this initial contact. Rather, your goal is twofold: (1) to establish a counseling relationship, and (2) to assess the couple's marital relationship.

Establishing a Counseling Relationship

In establishing a counseling or therapeutic relationship with counselees, *you are bonding or connecting with your clients on an emotional level.* This form of connecting is the first step in any counseling process. Some counselors refer to "establishing rapport." Others speak of "joining" with the couple. Your ultimate goal is to influence the couple in a way that will bring health to their relationship. This will necessitate some changes on their part that will likely be the result of your interventions. The right to intervene has to be earned, and you earn it through demonstrating that you care.

In establishing a therapeutic relationship, clients develop a growing sense of being cared for—not just as a reclamation project, but as people. Clients need to feel comfortable in your presence. They will if they know that you can be trusted, that confidentiality will be maintained, and that you are genuinely concerned for their well-being, regardless of what is shared in the sessions and in spite of the eventual outcome for the marriage.

To facilitate this atmosphere, you need to focus more on listening and asking questions than on instructing and confronting. There is a time and place for confrontation, but that time is not now. Your clients must sense a willingness on your part to listen without making hasty judgments. You want to know what happened. You want to know how each spouse perceives the situation. You want to know how each feels about the marriage and toward one another. And you want to know what each wants to see happen regarding the future of the marriage. You listen and you ask questions—not judgmentally or critically, but with concern. They have to know that you will be fair.

There will be times in future sessions when you will be directive and instructive. There will also be times when you will confront inappropriate behavior, both past and present. These times will be uncomfortable for everyone. But these times of intervention will be better received if you are perceived as someone who cares as opposed to someone who does not. If you do not earn the right to intervene—if a therapeutic bond is not established—your efforts will likely be ineffective.

Establishing the counseling relationship is not limited to solely connecting with the couple emotionally. *You will also want to establish some general parameters regarding the treatment process.* Couples need to know what they can expect from meeting with you.

Clients typically come to counseling in a confused state regarding expectations of the process. They either have no idea of what will take place or they are actually misinformed. You want to accomplish two objectives: (1) to bring them some relief from their confusion, and (2) to give them hope. Both of these overlap and are simultaneously accomplished by informing the couple of what is legitimate to expect—of what you will and will not do and of the structure of the restoration process. I want couples to leave the first session with the following realizations:

1. There will be little or no intervention during the first session, but that's okay. Couples may come to the first session with the anticipation that I am going to immediately do a significant intervention. I need to let them know that this is not the case. I inform them that I do not want to make any hasty judgments. I need to have all the facts before making any suggestions. I intend to become actively involved in their situation (and not be merely a listener or sounding board), but not during my first contact. This is my time to assess.

This clarification usually sufficiently disarms the couple. They are free to relax, and I am freed from the responsibility of doing something magical or miraculous. It also buys me some time. With the pressure to perform reduced, I am allowed opportunity to join. The more I can emotionally connect, the greater influence I can exert when the timing is right for intervening.

2. Healing will not be instantaneous. We live during a time of high technology and automation. Many of us have been raised with TV dinners and fast-food restaurants. We want to start out in houses comparable to those that took our parents twenty years to acquire. We want things done now as opposed to waiting. And we want any change in our lives to be as painless as possible. Is it any wonder that this mentality is carried over into our relationships?

Sometimes we even carry this mentality into our religion. We expect God to zap our marriages and miraculously heal the problems—to take away the pain and resentment and instantly restore the relationship to a predamaged state. That is not the way things work. Healing is possible, but it will not come instantaneously. Restoration will take some time. It is a process. It will come, but only as a result of following God's design for healing.

3. There is a predictable process for restoration. There is a plan for restoration that involves several steps. Each step has tasks to be accomplished and issues to be faced and resolved. Some of the steps will focus on the affair. Others will deal with the marriage. Regardless of the focus, none of the steps can be skipped. This would result in either an incomplete healing or a total block in the restoration of the marriage. Each step must be thoroughly completed.

Though the process of restoration is predictable, it is not easy and will take time. But they should have no fear—they will be guided along the way.

4. They can succeed—though they may not. Many relationships have come to this point of crisis. Some end in divorce. Other relationships manage to remain intact, but only the appearance of a marriage lives on. In these, there is no true healing to foster growth and intimacy. A final group of couples choose to put their relationships back together. They heal from the devastation and grow toward the type of relationship for which marriage was created.

There are many factors that seem to influence the determination of which group a particular couple will fall into. Most of these factors will be addressed during the counseling process. What is important to realize at this point is that successful restoration is within the reach of every couple. They do not have to become another statistic. Neither do they have to settle for the hollowness of a merely intact existence. They can have God's best.

5. *They will have to be willing to do what is necessary.* Having the potential to succeed, wanting to be successful, and actually succeeding, are three totally different things. Most couples have the potential. Many even have the desire for success. But those who actually achieve marital restoration will do so because they are willing to do what is necessary to make it happen.

As difficult and uncomfortable as the steps to restoration may be, successful couples face and resolve each issue. These couples do not wait to be magically or supernaturally zapped. Instead, they take responsibility for both their lives and their marriages and restore their relationships in love.

There is hope for restoration. It comes as a result of doing what is necessary. The couple has to be committed to working through the healing process—a process which has been given to us as a spiritual design.

Assessing the Couple's Marital Relationship

What is meant by "assess the couple's relationship"? Again, your task is twofold. First, you want to evaluate the general quality of their marriage. Second, you want to determine whether they have met the minimum prerequisites for beginning the restoration process.

Evaluating the Quality

In evaluating the quality of a couple's marriage, you are more interested in a historical description of what has transpired than you are in what may be presently occurring. You are witnessing the marriage at a point of crisis. There is probably a great deal of observable estrangement—emotional distance, intense hostility, argumentative or belligerent behavior—due to the recent events. However, what is presently occurring is not necessarily representative of the manner in which the couple has behaved throughout most of their years together. What has their marriage really been like?

As a result of this exploration, you want to be able to form some hypotheses. For instance, you want to have a sense of the *general level of well-being* at which this marriage has operated. Your concern is with both the quality of the relationship as well as the general level of health exhibited by each of the spouses personally. Has the marriage been healthy or unhealthy? What are the characteristics, both interpersonal and intrapersonal, which have led you to this conclusion? To what extent has unhealthiness been demonstrated?

Another area in which you want to form hypotheses is with *interferences*—the natural tendencies that stand in the way of a couple's developing the type of relationship for which marriage was created. What interferences have operated for the couple? Sometimes interferences are of a personal nature. For instance, the tendency to avoid conflict and the tendency to keep your feelings to yourself are interferences. These personality and behavioral characteristics interfere with the primary goal of marriage—to become more intimate. Other interferences can be of a contextual nature. For example, pressures from a stressful job can make it difficult to invest in a marriage the time and energy that are required. There are many kinds of interferences. What was operating in this marriage?

What was *each spouse's contribution* to the deterioration of the marriage? It may have been something that was done or that was left undone. Neglect can be as great a contribution to marital deterioration as any overt behavior. The focus here is upon the contributions of *each* spouse. This is not something that couples are adept at recognizing. Each can easily tell you the other's faults, but it is difficult for them to recognize their own. As the therapist you will need to make this kind of assessment.

There are several important reasons for evaluating the marriage in this regard. All will have implications for how you choose to intervene.

1. *Eventually, you will have to deal with the interferences.* This is not the time to deal with the factors that interfered with their marriage being what it was meant to be. Your task is first to deal with the crisis. However, once the issue of the affair has been successfully resolved, the couple will be redirected back to looking at their relationship. The interferences that have been a part of their marriage are still a part of their marriage. These interferences still need to be faced and resolved.

2. *You want a feel for the general level of emotional and relational well-being.* As a general rule, the healthier that an individual or relationship may be, the greater the potential for a positive response to therapy. Also, the general level of health has a great deal to do with the type of intervention that you may choose to exercise. Some individuals may be so unhealthy that intensive individual therapy will be necessary before any work regarding the marriage can be undertaken. For example, this might be the case with a significant personality disturbance, severe depression, or a major addiction.

Regarding the relationship, possibly it has been so unhealthy that the betrayal demonstrated by infidelity is not the major problem. For example, this might be the case with a repetitive history of abusive behavior on the part of one spouse coupled with codependency on the part of the other. Gaining a sense of the general emotional and relational health that has been present in the marriage can give you clear direction as to how and what you will need to do as a therapist.

3. *Identifying each spouse's contributions will reduce resistance to the restoration process.* In varying degrees, resistance of some form to the counseling process is encountered when attempting to restore a marriage that has deteriorated to a point of crisis. It is common for spouses (frequently both spouses) to project a great deal of blame upon the other spouse. From the offended we hear: "How could he/she do this to me?" From the offender we hear: "What I did was wrong, but he/she drove me to it!"

The tendency to blame, the attitude of justification, the failure to truly own or take responsibility for whatever part was played in the deterioration of the marriage and the precipitation of the crisis—all of these characteristics block the restoration process. Your desire is for there to be heartfelt remorse and genuine forgiveness. To move a couple to this place in the process may require confrontation on your part. Each spouse will need to be convinced of his or her personal contribution. Each will need to own his or her responsibility. This therapeutic maneuver will be aided by a thorough assessment on your part and identification of each spouse's contributions.

4. *Understanding the deterioration of the marriage will aid your attempt to move the focus of counseling from the affair to the relationship.* There are two parts of this marriage that need to be addressed: the crisis of betrayal and the overall relationship. The offended spouse and the offender have different and incomplete agendas when it comes to dealing with these two areas. The offended spouse wants to maintain the focus on the affair. The offender prefers to avoid dealing with either the affair or the relationship. Successful restoration will require that both be addressed.

To aid in dealing with the affair and moving on to the relationship, you will need to present a thorough rationale, presenting the affair in the light of marital deterioration—as symptomatic of a relationship that was not working. This does not legitimize or grant license to unacceptable behavior, but it does bring some understanding. The concept of affairs being symptomatic of faltering marriages will be thoroughly discussed in the next two chapters. Suffice it to say at this point that accomplishing this transition of focus (from the betrayal to the marital relationship) will be aided by understanding and a good rationale.

Determining Minimum Prerequisites

The real question that is being asked here is: "Is the couple ready to begin the process of restoring their marriage?" To aid in determining the couple's readiness, I have identified three prerequisites that must be met before the restoration process can begin.

A marriage with only the minimum prerequisites would be a pretty meager existence, but it is an acceptable place from which to start. It is important to note that even though the prerequisites are minimal, they are nonetheless *essential*—you cannot begin without them.

1. *The extramarital relationship has ended.* Ideally, this will be the case. If the affair is over, you will want some information regarding its resolution.

How did the relationship end?
Who decided it was over?
Was it your client who wanted out or was it the other person?
Were either or both of them forced to end the affair?
Are there still unresolved feelings of attachment for the other person?

Though it is best for the resolution of the extramarital relationship to be a past-tense reality, a present-tense action is acceptable. If the affair has not yet ended, but the offender is willing to immediately and completely sever his or her involvement, we can proceed with restoring the marriage. Rather than the statement, "The affair *has* ended," we now have, "The affair *is* ended." What we cannot work with is, "The affair *will* end." Past and present tenses are workable—future tense is not.

Sometimes offenders state a willingness to end the illicit aspects of the extramarital relationship but balk at the complete severing of any contact. They fail to understand the necessity for this behavior and suggest several reasons why contact should legitimately be maintained. From my perspective, there is *no* legitimate reason for maintaining contact. What follows are four of the more common reasons stated in an attempt to justify continued contact.

He/she has been a friend to me. Therefore, why can't the friendship continue even if the romance does not?

The likelihood that the relationship could continue as a friendship alone is extremely doubtful. There is an old adage that sums up my position: "Friends will often lovers become, but lovers friends never." This thinking is at best naive. Furthermore, graciousness of this enormity is far too much to expect from a previously betrayed spouse. Where is the offender's commitment? Is it to the other person or to the spouse?

I don't want to hurt him/her. Therefore, let's be compassionate.

We are responsible for what we do and for dealing with how we feel. We are not responsible for how others behave or how they feel. Doing what is right may be unpleasant. The goal in severing the former relationship is not to hurt, though that may be an outcome. The goal is to do what is right regardless of how this may affect others.

It is my responsibility to continue to have contact. Therefore, because of the requirements of a role or position, the offender needs to continue the execution of specific duties (for example, a pastor who feels responsible to continue counseling a woman with whom he has been involved).

When the boundary of the professional role was crossed (with the development of a romantic and emotional involvement), the right and privilege to continue these duties was lost. The role of responsibility, and any duties that may accompany this responsibility, can never again be regained.

Why do you want to be so vindictive toward him/her? Therefore, the expectation of complete severing of contact is wrong and maliciously motivated by the previously spurned spouse. This tactic places the problem squarely on the betrayed spouse, attempting to make the expectation that there be no contact seem unreasonable and vindictive.

This is a manipulative ploy. The offender is making judgments regarding motivation as opposed to describing behavior. It is not the goal of the betrayed spouse to be vindictive—regardless of what is said or how it may appear. The goal is for clear boundaries.

Whether the stated opposition to a complete severing of the relationship is a reason or an excuse is difficult to determine. A reason can be taken as honest concern. It is misplaced and needs to be challenged, but it is still honest. An excuse, on the other hand, is dishonest. It is the use of what appears to be a legitimate concern to cover an illegitimate desire. Usually an excuse actually represents a tendency to hang on to the illicit relationship, and this desire can prove to be problematic.

It can also be difficult to determine whether an extramarital relationship has truly been ended or not. There can be deception; there are no true guarantees. However, whereas we can take a risk with possibly being deceived, we cannot take a risk with blatant indecision. If the offender is not willing to completely sever the relationship with the other person, the couple is not ready to proceed with the restoration of their marriage. When this lack of commitment is present, you will need to look at an alternative course of action.

2. The offender is willing to work on the marriage. Jan came to my office in total distress. She had been referred by her pastor. The source of her distress was her marital relationship with Tom. They had been married for sixteen years. Those years had not been ideal. Tom had not been the easiest person to live with, but neither had their time together been terrible. At least that had been Jan's assessment, until she discovered Tom had betrayed the marriage.

After several weeks of Tom's denial, Jan finally confronted him with enough evidence to force an honest confession. It was then that Tom not only admitted to having an affair but also to having been terribly dissatisfied with their marriage for several years. Tom had a long list of complaints, which he willingly shared with Jan. He also went to great lengths explaining how he had finally found the woman of his dreams—a woman with whom he was hopelessly in love.

Tom never physically left the marriage, choosing instead to continue his affair without giving up any of the comforts of home. Jan never forced him to move out. She tolerated his blatant indiscretions hoping that something would happen to change his mind. Finally, what Jan had desperately longed for occurred. Tom stopped going out with the other woman. He began staying home at night and even started acting like his old self. So if Jan had gone through the crisis of discovery, the turmoil of Tom's blatancy, and his ultimate decision to return to the marriage without seeing a counselor, why was she seeking help now? And why was she experiencing so much distress? This was Jan's explanation:

I thought it was bad before—when Tom was involved with the other woman. It's even worse now that he's decided to stay. What makes it so frustrating is he's not willing to do anything to make things better. Whenever I try to talk to him about working on the marriage, he says, "Let's just put it all behind us and forget it ever happened. I want things to be just the way they were."

That really makes me angry! Things being "just the way they were" must not have been all that great. I mean, he was willing to leave me because of things being "just the way they were." He had a long list of complaints just a few months ago. So what's different now?

Tom isn't willing to see a counselor—not even once. He won't talk to me about the affair. I don't know how it got started or how it ended. He won't talk to me about the things that I didn't do or the things that I did but that he didn't like. I have no idea what needs to be different.

Tom refuses to get a medical checkup. I'm afraid he may have picked up some kind of sexually transmitted disease. You just never know these days. And he's not willing to change anything. He doesn't want to spend more time together. He doesn't want to spend less. He just doesn't seem to care one way or the other about anything. I'm totally frustrated.

Jan had the right to be frustrated. Things hadn't changed between Tom and her. If they weren't good before the affair, what is Jan supposed to assume about the condition of their relationship now? And what can be the predictable future for their marriage? Probably not good.

You have to wonder about Tom's motivation for returning to the marriage. What does he really want? Is his decision to stay based solely on personal convenience? It's difficult to say. What is clear is the lack of readiness for this couple to deal with restoring their marriage. Their relationship may remain intact, but it will not be reconciled unless both of them are committed to making some changes and to dealing with the marriage. In fact, not only will they fail to restore their relationship, you can predict that time will only mark a continued deterioration.

Restoration occurs when there are two willing participants, not just one. They both have to be willing to work on the marriage, whatever that may mean. This is a broad phrase and may mean different things for different couples, but without this willingness, readiness to proceed in restoration is absent. One willing spouse cannot bring restoration; there must be two.

3. The offender is willing to be involved in a counseling process. Technically, this prerequisite could fall under "working on the marriage," but it is so important that it warrants separate attention. Some couples may feel that they can make enough changes on their own and do not require outside help. I strongly question whether any marriage can healthily survive an affair without good professional intervention.

A marriage can survive betrayal; there is no question of that. But for it to do so, specific tasks must be accomplished. The things that need to happen for healing to take place are not likely to occur without outside prompting. Both spouses may want the relationship to be better and for the ordeal to be over, but they may not be excited about doing what is required for this to be accomplished—facing and dealing with one another (high emotional intensity), letting go, and moving on. These tasks are extremely difficult.

There are no Band-Aids in true restoration. Healing necessitates that the wound be thoroughly cleaned out. This cleansing requires both a knowledge of what is truly healthy and an intent to follow through.

I remember the words of one betrayed wife who came to see me after she and her husband had tried to put their marriage back together on their own. For some reason, they kept getting stuck. Sharon's countenance drastically changed from one of heaviness to relief when I told her that we would need to thoroughly discuss the affair—both her pain surrounding the betrayal and any questions that she may have of her husband regarding his extramarital involvement.

Whew! I thought something was wrong with me for wondering about what happened and wanting to know. Steve's been great since coming home. He's trying hard. But he doesn't want to talk about what happened. He says it will only hurt us. I'm trying to forget—but I just can't seem to let it go.

Some of my friends have been telling me that I'm only setting myself up for more pain—that I didn't really want to know. I've even been told that if I were Christian about the whole thing, I'd simply forgive and move on. Living each day with Steve's reluctance, I began to believe that they were right. This only increased my guilt. It's such a relief to know what is the right thing to do—but I don't think we can do it without help.

There is a lot of confusion regarding what does and does not need to occur for a relationship to heal. Even when confusion is dispelled, doing what you need to do is generally not an easy task. A counselor can help the couple learn what to do, choose to be healthy, and do what is necessary regardless of the personal discomfort. Without outside help, it is unlikely that the necessary tasks will be accomplished. Again, one spouse alone cannot make this happen. Unless both partners are willing to participate in the counseling process, the marriage is not ready to move toward restoration.

Factors Affecting Restoration

All restorations are difficult. However, a particular relationship can be either more or less difficult depending on the presence or absence of certain factors. Each of these factors can be presented in a continuum format, which will show how difficult the restoration process may be.

By evaluating the factors of the particular marriage that you are counseling, you will have a good picture of the task before you. The presence of any one of the most difficult factors could represent a significant problem in and of itself. When several are grouped together, the difficulty of your task increases considerably (see table next page).

The purpose of this exercise is neither to overwhelm you nor to give you unrealistic confidence. It is only to make you aware of the facts. Not every marriage is alike; neither is every case of betrayal. Though I am presenting a counseling model that identifies specific steps and tasks that must be accomplished, each relationship will present its own unique challenges.

I will proceed through this section of the book with the assumption that progress is being made at each step. Ideally, this will be the case. Things do not always progress ideally, however. Allowing for the fact that some relationships fail to move through the counseling process as smoothly as desired, I have included the third section of this book. In part 3 I will specifically address the five most common blocks or interferences to the restoration process. If things have stalled for you, the likely culprit will be found among those common blocks. You will need to resolve the obstruction before proceeding with restoration.

Final Thoughts

Marital restoration can get blocked at any time or point during the process. A husband may decide to drop out of counseling; a wife may find it too difficult to trust; resentment may become so much a part of their lives that neither will choose to let it go; or neither spouse may be able to offer the kind of forgiveness required of genuine reconciliation.

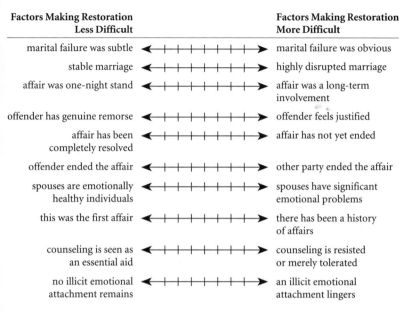

Factors Making Restoration Less Difficult		Factors Making Restoration More Difficult
marital failure was subtle	←——————→	marital failure was obvious
stable marriage	←——————→	highly disrupted marriage
affair was one-night stand	←——————→	affair was a long-term involvement
offender has genuine remorse	←——————→	offender feels justified
affair has been completely resolved	←——————→	affair has not yet ended
offender ended the affair	←——————→	other party ended the affair
spouses are emotionally healthy individuals	←——————→	spouses have significant emotional problems
this was the first affair	←——————→	there has been a history of affairs
counseling is seen as an essential aid	←——————→	counseling is resisted or merely tolerated
no illicit emotional attachment remains	←——————→	an illicit emotional attachment lingers

Where your intervention will lead and what may or may not emerge to block the restoration process is difficult to predict. One thing is certain, however: The process has to begin somewhere. For it to begin healthily, your clients must be ready to proceed.

One conjoint meeting may not give you enough information to accurately assess a couple's readiness. You may need the next two individual sessions to make a determination. But remember, though this is only a beginning, though much more will be required of each spouse for there to be true success, these minimum prerequisites must be met. They are essential, not optional. Without at least this amount of commitment from both spouses, you are not ready to begin marital restoration.

Quick-Scan 2

Things to remember about the first session

✓ Be sure the couple knows that you care.

✓ Explain what they can expect from counseling.

✓ Be sure to give them a reason to have hope.

✓ Obtain a feel for their individual and marital health.

✓ Assess their readiness to proceed (meeting minimum prerequisites):

- The extramarital relationship has ended.
- The offender is willing to work on the marriage.
- The offender is willing to be involved in the counseling process.

6
Preparing the Spouse

Preparing a couple for the restoration process is accomplished through individual counseling sessions as opposed to meeting with them conjointly. It makes no difference which spouse is seen first—the offender or the offended spouse. This is more a matter of personal preference and scheduling convenience. It is imperative, however, that both individual sessions be conducted prior to resuming conjoint contact.

The term *prepare* means "to get ready." *At this stage of counseling, you are getting the couple ready to deal with each other in a constructive and restorative manner.* You are preparing them to enter the restoration process. Adequate preparation will require that you deal with their *thinking.* Do they have correct perspectives, or will you need to challenge misperceptions and faulty information? You will also inform them of what each will need to *do.* Do they know what is required of restoration—that they will have to deal with each other? This may be the first time they have ever done this. Finally, you will need to work with their *attitude.* I like to take liberty with this term and broadly encompass what we think of as a person's heart. There is more than purely cognitive processes associated with an attitude; there is also emotion. An attitude shapes a person's perception and behavior. A right attitude is imperative for positive counseling progress.

There is commonality found in preparing both the offender and the offended spouse, but this commonality is in the broader categorical sense (what they think, what they do, and their attitudes). The specific issues needing to be addressed by offenders vary significantly from those needing to be addressed by their spouses. This particular chapter will focus on the issues of the offended spouse. In it, you will learn how to prepare the offended party to begin the restoration process.

A Right Attitude

A right attitude is one that possesses an appropriate balance of three ingredients: self-respect, honesty, and Christian love and forgiveness. The absence of any of these characteristics will prove problematic in counseling. A blending of all three is required for health.

Healthy Self-Respect

Self-respect addresses the issue of expectations and can be described with the question, What can a spouse legitimately expect from an offending partner? Some spouses feel they have the right to expect very little. Whether because of a faulty belief system, the insistence of an insensitive offender, or a generally low functioning self-worth, these spouses believe that they only have the right to expect what the offender is willing to offer. This is totally false. The offended spouse may not necessarily receive what is expected, but appropriate expectations are not only acceptable but necessary to true restoration. An offended spouse may legitimately expect to be told truthfully, "I was wrong," "I am sorry," "I am committed," and "I am changed or changing." (These statements are thoroughly examined in my book *A Change of Heart: Restoring Hope in Marriage.*) Unless these statements are evidenced in the offender's life, the relationship will not heal from the betrayal.

I have seen several instances where a healthy self-respect was lacking. The betrayed spouse held out for little more than the simple return of an errant partner. A lack of expectations may temporarily make it easier for an offender to return to a marriage, but the long-term consequences are negative. Your goal is for there to be genuine reconciliation and not merely to hold the marriage together. Whether motivated by dependency needs, fear, passivity, overresponsibility, or theological confusion, the outcome is the same—failing to maintain legitimate expectations prevents reconciliation and fosters the growth of resentment.

It is not un-Christian to expect an offender to admit wrongdoing. It is not un-Christian to expect an offender to feel genuine remorse for the pain he or she has caused. It is not un-Christian to expect an offender to make a commitment to the marriage and demonstrate the truthfulness of this commitment by meeting the minimum expectations for restoration. And it is not un-Christian to expect a change in unacceptable behavior. Though the presence of these expectations *is not* un-Christian, the absence of them *is* unhealthy.

Self-respect expects an offender to offer something back to the marriage. Legitimate expectations are both appropriate and essential. Some spouses who have been victimized by betrayal may need your encouragement in order to accept this concept and, once embraced, incorporate it into their overall attitude.

Honesty

Honesty addresses the issue of personal responsibility for the deterioration of the marriage and can be described with the question, What responsibility can the offended spouse own? Marital success and marital failure are both the result of combined efforts and rarely solely the achievement or fault of one spouse. There are instances where one spouse carries most of the responsibility, but seldom is there an all-or-nothing situation.

In dealing with the honesty issue, you want a spouse to accurately assess his or her own contributions to the marital failure. This requires a clear differentiation from the behavior of the offender. Regardless of what the offender did or did not do throughout the duration of the marriage, what has been the behavior of the spouse? The focus is upon personal historical behavior, and your goal is to cut through any denial that may be present.

Your theme is, "Accept what is yours to own—no more and no less." Finding this correct balance is not always an easy task. Offended spouses may fluctuate between two extreme and inaccurate poles. On one extreme is the attitude, "It was all *my* fault." From this vantage point, the spouse is taking on more responsibility than he or she should. This has significant implications when it comes to having legitimate expectations of the offender and in dealing with anger. A spouse who feels responsible for the offender's betrayal presents therapeutic difficulties in reconciliation.

The opposite extreme is reflected in the attitude, "It was all *his* fault." From this vantage point, the spouse is taking on *less* responsibility than she should. This usually results in a rigidity problem and complicates the forgiveness process. These spouses are frequently seen as self-righteous.

Do not confuse the acceptance of true contributions to the deterioration of a marriage with the granting of license for the offender's betrayal. Admitting to personal wrongdoing in no way legitimizes the offender's behavior. It may help us understand a little more clearly his or her motivation, but it does not justify the betrayal. The goal is to develop an honest attitude in the offended spouse. An honest attitude is one which owns what is legitimate to own—no more and no less.

Christian Love and Forgiveness

The final aspect of a right attitude addresses the issue of compassion and can be described by the question, What is a spouse willing to extend to the offender? Whereas a healthy self-respect focuses on what a spouse can expect to *receive*, Christian love and forgiveness gives attention to what a spouse can expect to *give*.

An offended spouse will feel legitimate pain from marital betrayal. It is appropriate to expect admission of wrongdoing and remorse from that offending behavior, but this is for the purpose of genuine reconciliation. The betrayal was a terrible thing, and the emotional and relational disruption prompted by this behavior has been horrendous, but an offended spouse cannot be permitted to remain in a position of focusing on the wrong that has been committed. The affair must be viewed, dealt with, and then released. There must be forgiveness. As I frequently share with my clients:

The betrayal was a terrible thing, but you cannot stay there. The command is to forgive. There can be no reconciliation without forgiveness. You will need to view your spouse with compassion. That is one of the characteristics which separates the Christian from the non-Christian. And it is how Jesus views us.

A sense of compassion, a healthy self-respect, an honest acceptance of personal responsibility—all of these cooperate to form a healthy and balanced attitude. It is the rare spouse who enters counseling with all of these accurately in place. More commonly, it becomes the task of the counselor to prepare the attitude of a betrayed spouse for the difficult work of marital restoration.

To Do or Not to Do

It is important that a spouse be given a complete understanding of what will have to be accomplished during the next several sessions. Your focus here is upon the specific resolution of the affair as opposed to dealing with the marriage in general. This focus can be clarified with the question, What will be required of the offended spouse in order to resolve the affair?

Two actions are required of couples for the effects of an affair to be resolved. First, the affair must be *discussed*. This will involve a thorough sharing of the offended spouse's feelings, including the pain which has been experienced. Second, there must be a complete *disclosure* by the offender of the events and activities of the extramarital relationship. This will include the answering of legitimate questions from the spouse. Both the discussion and the disclosure will be difficult.

Discussing the Affair

The goal of this discussion is not to emphasize events or answer questions—that will be handled during the disclosure. Rather, the focus here is an open and honest sharing of emotions. The offended spouse needs the opportunity to talk about the pain of the betrayal—the disappointment, rejection, embarrassment, humiliation, effects of feeling naive or being made a fool, or the loss of self-respect. In short, the offended spouse needs to get honest and bare all of his or her pent-up emotions.

Sharing of this nature can be quite intense. The fear of this intensity by both spouses is one of the reasons that thorough discussions frequently do not occur on their own. Though the discussion can be intense, it is necessary for resolution. Unless the offended spouse has an opportunity to express the pain, it will fester and act as a block to restoration. Also, many offenders need to hear the full extent of the effects of their actions in order to experience true remorse and honestly ask for forgiveness.

Some spouses fear their partner's reaction—that he may once again leave the marriage, that his feelings may be hurt, that he may get upset, that the relationship may be damaged. Others fear their own reaction—that once unleashed, their anger will be all-consuming and overwhelming. Still others fear that emoting like this is un-Christian or inappropriate. You will need to act as an enlightener and an encourager, challenging any obstacle that interferes with a spouse doing what needs to be done.

We will need to discuss the affair in detail, so be ready. It will be difficult, but it must be done. You must be prepared to be painfully honest.

The goal is to get it all out so we can let the affair go and move on. Share your pain. Tell why you hurt. It will be hard, but I will help you. I'll be there to guide you through.

The goal of discussing the affair is not to wallow in the pain. It is to face it, deal with it, let it go, and then move on. Many would prefer to simply skip to the final step of moving on. Others would rather stay and graze awhile in the pain, repeatedly berating the offender for his dastardly actions. Neither of these alternatives is helpful or productive. Skipping the discussion phase of restoration might appear to be the most comfortable course of action, but it is ineffective. Repeatedly bashing the offender is just as nonproductive as avoiding the discussion. It will serve only to drive an otherwise genuinely conciliatory spouse away from the marriage. A delicate balance must be found. Resistance on the part of either spouse to this balance may warrant intervention on your part. (This will be addressed in more detail in part 3.)

The awareness of the need, coupled with your willingness to support and guide the spouse in the process, is usually adequate preparation for the next session. With your encouragement, the spouse is generally ready to deal with the affair.

Full Disclosure

I have yet to counsel an offended spouse who did not have at least some unanswered questions regarding the events and activities of the betrayal. I am not referring to questions for which answers had already been given but which then became obsessions, with the offended spouse repetitively asking the same question. This obsessive and repetitive quality borders on harassment and is a totally different problem from that which is represented by the failure of full disclosure. My concern rests with the *unanswered* questions.

Sometimes questions go unanswered because they are never asked. They are ever present in the mind and serve as a constant reminder of the betrayal, yet they are never verbalized. Hesitancy to press the offender or even fear of what might be discovered may block communication. At other times, questions are asked but are totally resisted by an offender. For one reason or another—whether out of personal discomfort or the fear of upsetting a spouse—these questions are overtly and covertly ignored. Still other spouses never quite place their nagging inquisitiveness into concrete questions. They recognize an uneasiness surrounding the entire affair but cannot seem to bring themselves to face their own quandary.

Unanswered questions haunt a marriage; they act as hooks. Whereas a couple's goal is to place the affair in the past, unanswered questions serve only to anchor them to the betrayal, thus making it impossible to let go. All of a spouse's questions must be asked—and they also must be answered. It is only with complete disclosure that progress can be made.

As a counselor, you will need to inform the betrayed spouse of this necessity, help in the formulation of a thorough list of questions, and give assurances of your support during the conjoint session. Dealing with disclosure is an intense experience, but it is also necessary, survivable, and rewarding.

A Creative Leap

Your final goal in preparing a betrayed spouse to enter the restoration process is to lay the foundation for a cognitive creative leap. By this you will begin to challenge some of the spouse's thinking. As you will discover in the next chapter, the offender's thinking must also be challenged. However, the issue which presents difficulty for an offender is vastly different from that which frustrates an offended spouse.

The ultimate goal of your intervention in a betrayed marriage is not to resolve the affair. Successfully dealing with the betrayal is an essential first step, but it is not where your responsibilities end. You are trying to resolve the affair in order to enable the couple to then focus on an even greater problem— their relationship. Offended spouses are frequently more content to obsess about the dastardly deed than they are to actually face the problems of the marriage itself.

Neither spouse is yet ready to make the transition from focusing on the affair to attending to the marriage. However, it is your responsibility to prepare them both for that inevitability. With the offended spouse, this transition is accomplished by changing how the affair is viewed. Rather than allowing the total marital history to be condensed into a narrow sequence of events (the affair), a case is developed for viewing the affair within the context of the entire marriage. The affair is seen as a by-product of a faltering relationship instead of a solely malicious and unwarranted personal rejection. In what condition was the marriage before the affair occurred?

This represents quite a change in perception. You must challenge the tendency of the offended spouse to direct all the attention on the betrayal. A change of this magnitude—one which relegates the betrayal from the all-consuming focal point of a marriage to that of being merely a symptom of a greater problem (a faltering relationship)—is likely to be resisted.

You are not attempting to manipulate the betrayed spouse. Rather, you are attempting to bring reality into a narrowly focused mind-set. Most of the affairs that I treat are unpremeditated. This in no way absolves an offender from his or her inappropriate behavior. It is important to realize, however, that the clandestine intent to develop an illicit relationship is usually not present. These extramarital relationships develop accidentally. The fact that they developed at all usually indicates that the marriage was not what it needed to be.

The actual interferences that block the growth and development of a marriage will vary. So will the degree of shared responsibility for the failure and whether the deterioration is subtle and unrecognized or painfully obvious. Though the shapes and nuances of marital imperfection vary, what betrayed marriages seem to share in common is the presence of at least some degree of dissatisfaction. As with most characteristics of a marriage, the formation of this dissatisfaction is usually the result of contributions from *both* spouses. The marriage that *was* less than perfect (and from which an affair sprang up) is a marriage that still *is* less than perfect. This is the reality that you are attempting to instill.

In preparing a betrayed spouse for restoration, you want to encourage a realistic mind-set—one which may be contradictory to everything that the emotional system is communicating. It must also be a balanced mind-set. Whenever I begin laying the foundation for right thinking, I incorporate the following points.

1. Viewing the betrayal as symptomatic of a faltering marriage in no way legitimizes inappropriate behavior. There is no right reason for doing the wrong thing. Marital dissatisfaction, whether clearly recognized or subtly developed, does not justify extramarital behavior. We may gain a clearer understanding of what precipitated the affair, but the behavior itself was still inappropriate.

2. The pain caused by the betrayal is real. Regardless of the condition of the marriage or the motivation for the affair, the emotional pain from the betrayal is real. As such, it must be recognized, acknowledged, discussed, and resolved.

3. Affairs are usually symptomatic of a greater marital problem. We may not yet be aware of all of the factors that contributed to the faltering condition of the marriage, but we at least know that some problems were present. The affair was a poor solution for the marital dissatisfaction, but marital dissatisfaction was still the likely precipitant.

4. We need to deal with the affair. The emotional pain, the unanswered questions, the apprehensions regarding commitment and trust—all of these aspects of the affair must be dealt with and resolved. But our doing so is in order to allow us to move on. It is in getting past the affair and to the marriage that the real work of restoration begins.

5. The crisis that was precipitated by the affair will allow us the opportunity to deal with the more important historical problems of the relationship. We need to deal with what wasn't working in the marriage. The interferences that stood in the way of marital growth prior to the affair are still present. At least now there is opportunity, clarity, and motivation for dealing with these interferences. It is not your goal to allow the couple to repeat the errors of the past. So the marriage must be dealt with in order to offer the opportunity for an improved and enhanced relationship.

Most spouses will not leave your preparation session with a totally changed perspective of the marital betrayal, but at least you will have begun setting the stage for a transition. You will have further opportunities to reinforce this concept. At some point, however, a creative leap will have to be achieved if the marriage is to proceed toward restoration. The affair will have to be *released* so that the relationship can be *embraced.*

Quick-Scan 3

Things to remember about preparing the spouse

✓ Encourage a balanced attitude, which will be exhibited by the following characteristics:

- A healthy self-respect with legitimate expectations.
- A willingness to own personal contributions to the marital deterioration.
- A willingness to extend forgiveness.

✓ Explain what can be expected from the next several sessions.

- The affair will need to be discussed.
- Any remaining unanswered questions will need to be asked.
- Opportunity for genuine reconciliation will be provided.

✓ Lay foundation for the eventual change in focus from the act of betrayal to the marital relationship itself.

7

Preparing the Offender

As with betrayed spouses, offenders also need to be prepared for the work of restoration. They too have problems with their attitudes, thinking, and knowing exactly what they will be expected to do. However, the specific issues that present difficulty for offenders are of a different nature than those confronted by the spouse. Your success or lack thereof in challenging these unique issues will greatly determine the ultimate outcome of the counseling process for the couples with whom you work.

What Do You Really Think about Your Marriage?

During the initial conjoint session, offenders are generally more hesitant than their spouses to mention any historical dissatisfactions regarding their marriage. The absence of comments should not be interpreted as an absence of dissatisfaction. Most certainly there was some degree of dissatisfaction or there would not have been an affair. You need to know what the offender *really* thinks, not what he wants to project to you and to others. Your question should be, Where does he or she really stand on the historical quality of the marriage? You need to ascertain the offender's honest assessment of his or her marriage and then interject some balance.

Allow some time for the offender to describe the marriage. Let the themes of discontent emerge. If dissatisfactions do not readily come forth during the conversation, ask some leading questions:

What were the dissatisfactions?
Where were the disappointments?
What did your spouse do that frustrated you?

At this time, you are not to refute any claims as they are presented. You merely want the offender to give his or her account. Any confrontation of beliefs will occur once the marital portrait is complete, not before.

Operating under the assumption that marital failures are cooperative efforts, you are encouraging the offender to share his or her view of the marriage so that you can inject reality. The offender will undoubtedly be more descriptive regarding the spouse's role in the deterioration than his or her own role. It is your responsibility to balance the picture. In most instances, offender dissatisfactions rest with what a spouse either did or did not do or with what the marriage itself lacked. In any of these circumstances, ask yourself, What were the offender's contributions regarding these conditions? There is always something. You just need to know where to look and how to develop the counterrationale.

There are some themes that I frequently encounter in counseling. For example, it is common to hear one spouse complain that the other repetitively did something that he did not like. From his perspective, it was this behavior that led to a deterioration in their marriage. When asked what he did in an attempt to deal with his growing dissatisfaction, it is just as common to get a blank stare, a long silent pause, or an "I don't know" in response.

Let me get this straight, Jeff. For years, you felt that your wife put your children's needs over your own—that you were discounted in your own home. Yet, though your resentment continued to increase, you did nothing to deal with this growing dissatisfaction.

What did you expect from Phyllis? Did you expect her to read your mind? Was she just supposed to know that you were dissatisfied? Why did you not bring this to her attention? Do you not see your role in this deterioration—that your failure to deal with your dissatisfaction was your contribution to the marital failure?

It is also common to hear complaints regarding the lack of closeness in a marriage. Instead of an intimate and bonded relationship, there was distance. Sometimes the couple has subtly drifted apart, each so preoccupied with other goals and activities that they failed to notice the growing void in their relationship. In other relationships, the absence of closeness was far more apparent. Still, little was done to remedy the problem. The irony of this situation is that offenders will invariably place the greater amount of blame for failing to recognize and correct this lack of intimacy on their spouse.

If I understand you correctly, you just woke up one morning to the realization that, after fifteen years of marriage, you didn't really know this person lying next to you in bed. There was no closeness, no intimacy, no special feeling. At one time there had been passion, but it was no longer there. And you didn't know whether you could live the rest of your life in that kind of a marriage.

Marriages do not move from being a close, intimate, bonded relationship to an emotional wasteland in one day. Where were you during those fifteen years? When did it begin to go bad? What did you do to build this relationship? (Usually, I get more stares, silent pauses, and "nothing's" at this point.)

Don't you see? If there was this much void in your marriage, you definitely contributed to its presence. If through no other means than by doing nothing, you contributed.

I am not trying to dispute offender concerns regarding marital dissatisfaction. The complaints may be quite legitimate. I am only attempting to bring him to a point of balanced thinking. His spouse may have erred, *but so did he.* It is the realization of personal contribution that brings balance.

After listening to an offender's story, I look for a seam in his defenses—a place for me to slip through and begin to undermine his skewed perspective. The particulars will vary from relationship to relationship, but each intervention must emphasize personal responsibility. "What did *you* do?" Was it a failure to constructively deal with dissatisfaction? Was it a failure to invest in the marriage? Was it faulty and immature expectations of the relationship? Whatever is discovered, balance is brought to the offender's thinking by confronting him with his own failed responsibility.

Attitude Check

This was my first meeting with Doug by himself. I had seen Amy and him together during the initial conjoint session and had already met individually with Amy to help prepare her for what was to come. She had voiced some apprehensions regarding future sessions. Amy had some unanswered questions pertaining to the affair and was concerned whether Doug would be willing to deal with the betrayal—in either discussion or disclosure. "He's such a private person," she said.

Doug and Amy were very different people; this was obvious from our first encounter. Their natural differences, and the problems these caused, were frequently cited by both Doug and Amy as they shared with me some of the descriptive facts of the marital history. Conjointly, they described how their energy levels were at opposite poles with Amy possessing a calmer disposition and enjoying a more mundane existence. She liked evenings at home either in front of the television or curled up with a good book. "Doug kids me about being dull." Doug was the active and energetic spouse. He was always on the go or busy with some project. In our individual session, Amy shared how their varied interests made it easy for them to drift apart. Amy liked the tamer side of life whereas Doug was a rugged outdoorsman. He hunted, fished, camped, skied, and was a proficient scuba diver—not just occasionally, but with a passion. Because none of these passions were held in common, Doug usually involved other friends in his activities. His being gone so often served as just another point of marital contention.

So as Doug and I spoke, I heard more examples of how their different interests seemed to work against closeness as opposed to aiding the marriage. I recognized the difficulty and so did they. There was no discrepancy in the reporting of facts, and this differentness was obviously an issue to be reckoned with at a later point in the restoration process. What struck me at this point, however, was not the statement of facts, but an underlying tone that seemed to be coming from Doug's presentation.

Amy and I have always had different interests. She likes to be in the house—I like to be outside. She likes to watch TV—I like to be doing something. We have never been in sync.

I know that I shouldn't have gotten involved with Betty. But it was such a natural thing. Betty liked doing all the things I did. If Amy hadn't wanted me to look elsewhere, she should have shown more interest in the things that were important to me.

I did not dispute the facts or events of Doug and Amy's marriage. Nor did I dispute the realistic difficulties inherent in personal differences. What did concern me was the veiled implication being expressed by Doug. I detected an attitude of *justification.* Doug was suggesting that, due to the particular set of circumstances in which he found himself, his inappropriate behavior was somewhat justified and, therefore, excusable.

Granted, the natural differences that existed between Doug and Amy, and their failure to successfully deal with these differences, may help *explain* how their marriage drifted apart, but they in no way justify Doug's inappropriate behavior. *Understanding does not grant license.* Doug cannot excuse his poor behavior because of the supposed lacks in either his spouse or his marriage.

It is not unusual for offenders to come to counseling with at least some degree of an attitude problem. Having a bad attitude is not ideal, but it does not mean that counseling will be futile. Hopefully, the errant attitude can be identified, pointed out, challenged, corrected, and replaced with a more appropriate perspective. If the bad attitude is severe, or if it persists past a few sessions, another course of action will have to be undertaken before any progress in restoration can be achieved. (This will be thoroughly addressed in part 3.)

A good attitude is one that leads toward reconciliation. It will include at least the core elements of (1) acceptance of personal responsibility of wrongdoing and (2) genuine remorse. There will also be more present than just the willingness to do what is right, which is primarily a behavioral component and can be the product of a well-developed sense of responsibility alone. You can work with a willingness to be responsible, but it is far preferable for an offender to also have the desire to do what is right. This reflects more of an emotional element. The lack of desire can be due to the presence of a bad attitude.

Bad attitudes come in several variations. Watch for them. Each can prove to be a hindrance to counseling progress if allowed to persist. It is your responsibility to bring this interfering attitude to light, thus allowing the possibility of dissipation. The following are the bad attitudes which I most frequently encounter.

Justification

This attitude was illustrated by Doug and Amy's situation. Though Doug was the offender, he felt his inappropriate behavior was at least in part legitimized because of Amy's deficiencies.

Resentment

This attitude is similar to justification in that it is an offender's response to a spouse's historical marital behavior. With this variation, the offender harbors resentment toward his spouse for what he believes to be significant mistreatment. Although the resentful offender does not believe that this mistreatment legitimized the affair his deep-seated bitterness toward his spouse does block his ability to cooperate with the restoration process.

Control

This attitude reflects more of a long-standing personality tendency within the offender than it does any reaction to the previous behavior of a spouse. Some people have difficulty responding to the expectations of others and view these as demands. Cooperation and mutuality are seen as activities that place them under the authority of others—and this will not be tolerated. By personality, these offenders are more than willing *to* control, but they will not *be* controlled. Having to do anything that they do not want to do, no matter how necessary and legitimate this expectation may be, is viewed as being equivalent to being controlled.

Attachment

This particular attitude represents an offender's feelings toward the person with whom he had the affair. There are still feelings of caring. This continued attachment presents a problem because the offender's loyalty is divided. He still feels pulled out of the marriage. It is difficult to move in two directions at once. The continued attachment to the other person hinders investment in the spouse and the restoration process.

Though it is not unusual to encounter some degree of resistance with offenders, it is hoped that the attitudinal aspects will either be minimal in severity or brief in longevity. If not, these bad attitudes will warrant more intensive attention.

What You Will Have to Do

The final area of preparation deals with what will be required of an offender during the restoration process. Recognizing that an offender's preferred position is to not deal with the affair at all, your revelation may come as quite a shock. As you work through the list of do's, be sure to emphasize that restoration will not occur unless each of these is completed. This may prove to be sufficient motivation for an offender to do what he would otherwise prefer to avoid.

Discuss the Affair

There will be a discussion, though the offender will probably do far more listening than he will talking. He will hear about hurt and frustration. He will hear how it felt to be rejected and betrayed. He will listen to stories of embarrassing incidents, of trying to comfort confused children, of episodes of despair and disbelief. In short, he will hear of his spouse's pain.

The discussion will be uncomfortable. There will be tears. There will be raised voices. There will be intense emotions. Some offenders fear this aspect of restoration more than any other. Still, it is necessary. The offender needs to hear of the pain, and the offended spouse needs to share it. The pain must be shared, and it must be heard—truly heard—in order for it to be released.

The goal is not for the couple to remain in this pain, but neither is it the goal to either deny or avoid its presence. The pain must be faced, no matter how difficult or uncomfortable for either spouse, in order for healing to begin. Assure the offender of both the necessity of this process and the limits which pertain to it. This will not be the beginning of a long series of offender-bashing experiences. There will be an appropriate balance found and adhered to. You are there to see that appropriateness is maintained.

Offer Complete Disclosure

Offenders generally do not want to disclose pertinent details regarding the affair. If the other person is unknown, they do not wish to name him or her. There are many questions prompted by betrayal—most of which go unanswered: How and when did they meet? Who initiated the development of the relationship? When did it turn romantic? What was the intent? Etc.

Offenders have several rationales they use to oppose the disclosure of pertinent details. The most-used rationale even has a noble sound: "I do not want to cause my spouse any more pain." Though there may be a degree of truth to this statement, truer motivation more often rests with self-protection as opposed to overprotection. Fear seems to be at the core of an offender's preference to not disclose details.

Fear of retribution from either the spouse or the other party.

Fear of further embarrassment.

Fear of further complications in life, whether in a social context or in the career.

Fear of legal ramifications if marital restoration fails.

Fear of personal discomfort as the information is disclosed.

Fear of how the offender will appear if everything is known.

Fear of inflicting more pain on an already beleaguered spouse.

All of these fears support an offender's basic belief that the less said the better.

Though there may be some legitimacy associated with these fears, restoration requires that complete disclosure occur. It is also important to assure the offender that the goal of the disclosure is not to do harm. Rather, it is an attempt, as temporarily painful and uncomfortable as it may be, to squarely face the betrayal so that it can then be released. Your goal is to answer all of the questions, once and for all, so that the marriage can move on to more important business. With this broader perspective, offenders usually prove to be more willing participants.

Reconcile the Marriage

The sharing of pain is meant to bring more than a cathartic experience for the spouse. It also offers an opportunity for genuine reconciliation. The offender needs a fresh awareness of how his behavior impacted the lives of others. Betrayal is a terrible thing. It causes chaos, disruption, and emotional turmoil. For reconciliation to occur, an offender needs to gain a sense of the pain that his behavior caused for his spouse.

In preparing the offender, you will want to give him an appreciation for reconciliation as a process and for the role he must play. He will be required to say, "What I did was wrong." This involves a sincere acceptance of personal responsibility. There is no room here for placing blame on anyone or anything else. He did wrong and admits it.

The offender will also be required to say, "I am sorry." This is far more than a flippant statement; genuine remorse is deeply emotional. In biblical examples, it is evidenced by brokenness and a contrite spirit (see Ps. 51:17; Matt. 26:75). The offended spouse's sharing her pain frequently awakens the offender to the reality of the hurt he has inflicted, which can result in genuine remorse.

Finally, the offender will be required to say, "I am committed." By this he reaffirms his allegiance to the marriage both as an *institution* and as a *relationship*. The original commitment to marriage as an institution was stated in the marriage vows, "so long as you both shall live." This speaks to the issue of intactness. Marriage as a relationship was committed to in the rest of the vows: "to love, comfort, honor, cherish, keep, and to forsake all others. . . ." Commitment to the relationship will require different things from different people. However, each offender must express a willingness to do whatever it takes.

These are the essentials for genuine reconciliation. There are no shortcuts. Without these essentials, the restoration stalls. "This is what will need to happen. Are you ready?"

Deal with Interferences

Some offenders come to counseling with the perception that after only a few sessions, things will be back to normal in their marriages. That is an erroneous assumption. First of all, if everything progresses smoothly, it will take several sessions to even resolve the betrayal itself. Second, getting things back to normal is not an ideal goal. Things being normal allowed for the development of an affair. Does it seem reasonable for a couple to even desire to return to such a place? I don't think so.

The betrayal has created some problems for the relationship. Whatever interferences were present before the affair are still present, even though the affair has ended. If these interferences created a problem earlier in the relationship, they will again. The particular interferences will vary from couple to couple, but it is always necessary to identify and resolve each one. The offender must be committed to dealing with his marriage, whatever that may mean, in order to bring full restoration. This will require that he be ready to ultimately (after the affair has been resolved) deal with the interferences in his marriage. Anything short of this will destine his relationship to being only back to normal—and this is one time when normal is not good enough.

Quick-Scan 4

Things to remember about preparing the offender

✓ Determine the offender's honest assessment of his or her marriage.

✓ Bring balance to the perception of the marital deterioration by identifying personal contributions.

✓ Watch for and challenge any bad attitudes.

- justification
- resentment
- control
- attachment

✓ Explain what can be expected from the next several sessions.

- The affair will need to be discussed.
- Any remaining questions that the spouse may have will need to be answered.
- Opportunity for genuine reconciliation will be presented.

✓ Lay foundation for continuing in therapy past the resolution of the affair.

8

Reconciling the Marriage

To this point in the counseling process, everything has been fairly structured. The first session found you meeting with the couple and making a greater effort at establishing an emotional bond and therapeutic relationship than attempting any form of intervention. The next two sessions were preparatory in nature. Though there are no two spouses (nor marriages for that matter) entirely alike, the respective offender and offended spouse agendas for these sessions are fairly predictable. You assess where the spouses are, challenge the inappropriate aspects, encourage the appropriate, and inform them of what will be required if restoration is to be attained. Short, direct, to the point—your role has been clearly laid out. Now, however, things begin to change.

In essence, the first three sessions have established the foundation for the couple to actually resolve the betrayal and to move on to restoring their marriage. You are now ready to face the affair, deal with the important issue of reconciling the marriage, and dispense with any remaining remnants of the betrayal through the act of disclosure (discussing any unanswered questions). Though this to-do list may have the appearance of structure, how it is actually accomplished is extremely variable.

There is no set order in which to resolve these issues. You do not have to deal with the affair first, followed by reconciliation, and then end with disclosure. The order of resolution is optional. You could begin with disclosure and then move to the others. You may even find that, in dealing with one area, you actually deal with the others as well. Neither is there a prescribed length of time to be spent with these issues. Though not probable, it is possible to resolve all three tasks in a single session. This would suggest a high degree of readiness on the part of a couple. It is far more likely for the process to involve two or three sessions. Much of the variability rests with what the couple is presenting (how well they have already resolved these issues) and your own personal counseling style. The rule of thumb is this: Do what is warranted.

I view this phase of the restoration process as turning the corner. The couple needs to make a transition from focusing on the betrayal to dealing with their marriage. I normally allow two sessions to accomplish this change in focus. Sometimes we will carry it over to a third meeting. However, if the transition from the betrayal to the relationship has not been accomplished in that period of time, I begin to search for blocks to restoration. What is preventing them from moving on? If a couple is stuck in the affair, there is a reason, and your role as a counselor is to discover the particular hindrance and resolve it. (This is the subject matter of part 3.)

When turning the corner, I help a couple talk about the affair and reconcile their relationship during the same session. These two activities are easily combined and actually go together fairly naturally. Talking about the pain of betrayal and all of the problems precipitated by the affair seems to lead to offenders saying, "I'm sorry," and spouses replying, "I forgive you." This may be the first discussion of this type for the couple—the first attempt at true reconciliation. But even if reconciliation has already been achieved, I at least want confirmation of that fact. The disclosure of the events of the betrayal and dealing with unanswered questions is usually accomplished during a session clearly devoted to that purpose.

Though the next two chapters will deal with the talking, reconciling, and disclosure issues in a stated order, do not feel constrained to follow this sequence. Do what is warranted by your particular situation. Switch the order, shorten or lengthen the amount of time spent, discuss each issue separately, or let each overlap with the others. Do what works for you and the couples with whom you are counseling. Just be sure that all of these issues are resolved. You do not want to leave any reason for clinging to the past.

Talking

For many couples, talking about the affair has been taboo. There has been too much tension associated with the events of the betrayal to allow easy discussion. This does not mean that it has not occupied their thoughts. In fact, the mental anguish and absorption of thoughts has probably been overwhelming. However, the likelihood that a thorough and constructive discussion of feelings and attitudes regarding the betrayal has already occurred is doubtful. Now is the time to talk!

Couples need to talk about the betrayal so that they can let it go. The memory of the affair does not need to occupy every waking moment, but until it is discussed, it probably will. Talking about the betrayal will mean different things for the offended spouse than the offender, both in goals and roles. For the offended party, it will be a time to vent. For the offender, it will be a time to listen—to honestly hear and respond to the pain of a betrayed spouse. This time of emotional release will occur in the safe context of the counseling office. As a counselor, you will attempt to move the discussion toward a point of reconciliation for the couple.

The offended spouse will do most of the talking. The offender should already be prepared for this. You will encourage the talking process by (1) indicating the parameters of the session, (2) reemphasizing the need for the resolution of the affair, and (3) prompting each spouse with specific statements.

Initial Prompter Statements

Your initial instructions are directed to the offended spouse. Your encouragement is for him or her to vent.

- "Talk to Bob about how it made you feel when you learned of the betrayal."
- "Tell Bob how you feel now."

After a significant time of venting, you might ask whether the offender is actually hearing what his spouse is saying.

- "What are you hearing Alice say? Are you hearing more than words? Are you sensing her pain? Tell her about it."

Transitional Prompter Statements

After an ample time of venting and listening, you want the couple to embrace a reconciliatory posture. You aid in this transition by changing the direction of their discussion. Here are some statements you may wish to use with the offended spouse:

- "Tell Bob what you need to own regarding your marriage. What have been your contributions to the marital failure?"
- "Tell Bob what you want to see happen for this marriage."
- "Tell Bob what you need from him right now for the two of you to put this betrayal in the past and to enable you both to move on."

After the spouse has had the opportunity to address his or her partner regarding personal ownership and needs, the offender can be directed with the following statements:

- "Tell Alice what you can own. For what can you assume responsibility? What have you done wrong?"
- "What do you want to tell her?" (I'm sorry. Will you forgive me?)

Can you see the flow of the talking phase? The betrayal needs to move from the taboo status to being addressed, but it does not need to become a permanent fixture. Betrayal is addressed in order for it to be released. The offended spouse needs to vent—to express the pain. The offender needs to hear it—to validate the pain and to experience remorse. Both need to move toward a point of reconciliation where you will clearly hear statements like:

I was wrong.
I am sorry.
I am committed.
You are forgiven.

Your goal in allowing the couple to talk is to move them to this point of reconciliation. Once this has occurred, there is no longer any reason to return to the affair. It is a part of their past. They choose to let it go in order to embrace the present and the future. When it appears that they are ready to move on, you can bring closure to this aspect of the restoration with a simple statement: "Let's move on. We do not need to discuss this any more."

A Clean Reconciliation

The Robertsons were older than most of the couples I see for counseling. They had been married nearly forty years, and John was strongly considering an early retirement. Their marriage had been unremarkable; there was nothing to distinguish it from any other normal relationship. John and Martha had been childhood sweethearts and married after high school. John worked in the printing industry while Martha stayed at home and raised three children. When their youngest child entered high school, Martha found a job. From her perspective, it seemed like the only reasonable thing to do. After all, "I had to do something with my time." What originally began as a productive utilization of Martha's time gradually made a transition into a significant career. Martha was good at what she did, and success has a way of changing priorities.

After thirty years of marriage and with three grown children, the Robertsons were a picture of success and normality. There was no hostility, no bickering. Just the opposite—everything was calm and pleasant. John did his thing, and Martha did hers. The only problem with this picture of perfection was the absence of *theirs*. There really wasn't much marital investment taking place—nothing to hold this couple together.

The drifting apart probably began much earlier in their marriage than when Martha went to work. John had always been invested in his career, and Martha found three active children to be more than a minor preoccupation. But going to work—and then the job becoming a successful career—only exacerbated an already developing void in their marriage. Emotional closeness all but disappeared between them. That was when a significant other entered the picture for John.

There had been signs that things were not what they needed to be. John had noticed the void, but when he mentioned to Martha the emotional distance that he was sensing, it was as if she did not really hear him. The marriage had drifted for many years. Both Martha and John had contributed to the depleted condition of their relationship, but John began to feel as though the void in their relationship was of more concern to him than it was to Martha. From his vantage point, she was far too busy meeting the needs of those with whom she worked to attend to anyone else's, especially his. With an underlying core of resentment, John began responding to the affections of a younger coworker.

We were now two years further down the marital path. The affair had been discovered a month earlier. Everyone was shocked. There was an immediate crisis. Martha was upset and so was John. The children, now with families of their own, first talked to Mom and then to Dad. Their pastor got involved as did other Christian friends. There was talk of divorce, talk of separation, and finally talk of staying together. John and Martha had done more real talking during the last month than they had in the previous ten years combined. But now they were sitting in my office.

I've done a bad thing. If you had asked me several years ago if I would ever consider having an affair, I would have laughed in your face. Then I went ahead and did the very thing that I despise.

I was lonely, and I was a little miffed at Martha. It didn't seem to make much difference to her that I was dissatisfied with what was happening in our marriage. Still, that doesn't justify what I did. It helps me to understand my actions, but it doesn't make what I did right.

What happened to our marriage was as much my fault as it was Martha's. I guess we were both just too busy with less important things and totally neglected the things that really matter.

I messed up, and I'm sorry. I've told Martha that. I hope she can forgive me. She says she has, but I've done a lot to be for-given for. All I want is a chance to make it up to her. We can have a good life together—I know we can. I just need a chance.

John's words were filled with emotion. He was somewhat anxious as he spoke. There seemed to be a genuineness in his remorse for what he had done and the pain it had caused. Though he alluded to the marriage as being less than perfect,

John did not cling to that imperfection as a justification for his actions. He was in my office to officially make a plea for the continuance of his marriage and not to shift the blame or dodge personal responsibility.

Martha's voice was calmer than John's, but she seemed just as genuine:

> I was totally surprised when I learned of the affair. I had had no idea that anything was going on. Ironically, after living through the first week or two of the shock, it was this realization—that I had not had a clue—that really forced me to look at the desperate condition of our marriage and what I had done to help create it.
>
> I should have known something was going on, but I didn't. I was so distant from John—so out of touch—and had been for years. I was used to the distance, but that's no excuse. John didn't have the right to do what he did. The thought of it still hurts me. But it wasn't all his fault.
>
> I've forgiven him for what he did. I still have some problems with my emotions. I'm doing the best I can right now, but I've also had to ask his forgiveness—forgiveness for neglecting him and our marriage, and forgiveness for not listening when he tried to deal with me about his concerns.
>
> I believe we've both done *wrong* and now we're both trying to do *right*. It's going to take some time, but I think we can make it work.

We'll return to the Robertsons a little later, but based on their words, it appeared as though I was dealing with a *clean* reconciliation.

The familiar biblical story of the prodigal son (see Luke 15:11–32) is an illustration of what I mean by a *clean reconciliation*. In this example, there is an offender—an errant one—who clearly comes to himself. The son takes responsibility for his behavior, admits that he has been wrong, and feels authentic remorse for his actions. His behavior is changed and forgiveness is sought for past offenses. There is also one who is offended—one who has been wronged—yet who is clearly willing to forgive his transgressor. The father lovingly accepts back his errant son, and the result is healing for their relationship.

It is easy to change the players illustrated in the story of the prodigal son, while maintaining the two roles of an offender and the one offended, and project this situation into the realm of marital betrayal. In an analogy of this type, the errant son would be portrayed by an adulterous spouse who, after coming to himself, leaves the illicit relationship to return home. Totally owning the responsibility for his behavior, and with genuine remorse for the pain he has inflicted, he asks the forgiveness of his spouse. The role of the prodigal's father is then played by the offended spouse who lovingly and faithfully forgives the errant one and accepts him back. The reconciliation of this betrayed marriage is clean; there is total acceptance of responsibility and total forgiveness. One spouse is clearly an offender and the other clearly offended—one has the appearance of being bad and the other the appearance of being good.

Within the realm of clean reconciliations, there is another variation that warrants our attention. The scenario established by the story of the prodigal, and repeated in our analogy of a betrayed marriage, clearly represents errancy as a black-and-white issue. One player was clearly in the wrong and the other was clearly in the right. In the marriages with which I counsel, I see very little color that is truly black or white. Rather, I see varying shades of gray.

This was the case with the Robertsons. There was an offender—one who had clearly behaved inappropriately. John recognized his errancy. He then took responsibility for his actions rather than searching for excuses. John was remorseful and asked Martha's forgiveness. Martha, the offended spouse, willingly forgave John. To this point there is no observable difference in the two variations. What happened next, however, offers the distinguishing characteristic. Martha then took responsibility for her own contributions to the marital failure. There were things that she needed to own. Like John, she too needed to admit fault, indicate her remorse, and ask her spouse's forgiveness.

None of what Martha did during the course of her marriage justified John's behavior. Nothing she did gave him permission to be unfaithful. Her contributions help us to understand the deterioration of their relationship, but they in no way justify infidelity. Yet, her insensitivity to John's needs and neglect of their marriage were also wrong. Martha had failed John. And for her part in the marital deterioration, Martha needed John's forgiveness.

The Robertsons had a clean reconciliation. Unlike the story of the prodigal, what made it clean was not a sharp contrast between right and wrong demonstrated by either John or Martha. As it turned out, the distinctions between the two were not as sharp as we would like to believe. What made their reconciliation clean was the willingness with which each embraced reality. Both John and Martha honestly faced their situation and themselves and took responsibility for what they found. John was sorry for his infidelity, and Martha was sorry for her insensitivity. From this foundation of their mutual need of forgiveness, John and Martha were able to genuinely reconcile their relationship. Nothing was left un-owned. There were no emotional loose ends. What followed was a beautiful restoration of their marriage.

Sloppy Reconciliations

Relationships characterized by clean reconciliations recover well. Much like physical wounds that are thoroughly cleansed, there is little to impede the natural healing process. Contrast this with sloppy reconciliations.

If a clean reconciliation is characterized by complete ownership of personal responsibility for wrongdoing (by both spouses if appropriate), a sloppy reconciliation is represented by a lesser acceptance of personal responsibility. This could be demonstrated by any one of several attitudes. An offender may possess a sense of lingering justification: "I did wrong, but it's really your fault." Another offender may possess an attitude of anger or resentment: "I did wrong, but I was also hurt by our marriage." A betrayed spouse may cling to the travesty of the offense: "How could you ever have done such a terrible thing to me? I was the perfect wife, yet this is how you repay me!"

The following diagram visually represents the difference between clean and sloppy reconciliations. The true distinction hinges on an individual's willingness to accept personal responsibility for his or her behavior, whether as an offender or an offended spouse.

Total Acceptance   Nonacceptance
1——2——3——4——5——6——7——8——9——10
Behavioral Responsibility in Marriage

A spouse's status on the continuum is determined by a combination of what is *said* and what is *believed*. A clean reconciliation occurs when a spouse says he was wrong and totally believes it. He would score one, totally accepting responsibility for his behavior. Scores in the two to five range would represent sloppy reconciliations. There is an acceptance of some responsibility, but in his mind someone or something else is still at least partially responsible for his inappropriate behavior. Spouses who fall to the right of the continuum (six to ten) do not even qualify for sloppy reconciliations.

It could be argued that there is no such thing as a sloppy reconciliation. Couples either truly reconcile or they do not. In the long run, this is true. There is no reconciliation without true reconciliation. In the short run—the early stages of therapeutic intervention—attitudes that reflect a less than total acceptance of personal responsibility can be worked with. Marginal acceptance of responsibility is not the ultimate goal, but it can be a beginning point. Though spouses to the extreme right of the continuum have little or nothing to offer to the therapeutic process, a marginal position is at least initially acceptable. Through the counseling process, the desired goal will be to move to honest acceptance of responsibility; the eventual success of counseling will hinge on ultimately making this transition.

Quick-Scan 5

Things to remember in bringing reconciliation

✓ Allow the couple to talk about the betrayal.

- Provide a safe context for both spouses to share.
- Encourage the offended spouse to vent.
- Encourage the offender to listen.

✓ Allow an opportunity for genuine reconciliation.

- Has the offender come to himself as exhibited by, "I'm wrong"; "I'm sorry"; "I'm committed"; and "I'm changing."
- Has the offender asked to be forgiven?
- Has the offended spouse extended forgiveness?
- Is there a need for mutual forgiveness?

✓ Is the reconciliation clean or sloppy?

9

Full Disclosure

The Petersons were a military couple. By necessity, Mark was away from home for weeks and even months at a time. As long as they were together, the marriage seemed to operate perfectly. The times of separation, however, were difficult. Kathy would soon miss Mark's presence in her life and grow lonely. Though he called every week or two, Mark seldom wrote to Kathy. This bothered her, but Kathy's complaints and requests went unheeded. Mark just wasn't much of a writer. Still, even with Mark's shortcoming, the marriage managed to move along in an acceptable fashion—that is, until Mark's last trip.

Mark was sent away for twelve weeks of specialized training. This separation began like all the others. Mark called weekly, but he would not write. As frustrating as Kathy found this to be, she was growing to accept Mark's neglect as reality. After six weeks, however, Kathy began to sense that there was something different about this separation. When Mark called, he seemed to be more emotionally distant than usual, and conversations grew stilted and uncomfortable. Kathy's first thought was that Mark was just tired. She knew that the training was demanding, but as the weeks passed, she began to suspect that something else might be happening. Mark's suggestion that she remain at home instead of coming to his graduation only heightened Kathy's suspicions. She was determined to go.

The specialized training had been coeducational, drawing together both men and women from across the United States. It had been especially intensive, forcing groups of cohorts to quickly form close friendships. Kathy arrived a day prior to the ceremony, which allowed Mark an opportunity to introduce her to his friends at an informal party scheduled on the eve of graduation. Although everyone was cordial, there was a strangeness in the relationships. Kathy felt like an intruder. It was as if everyone knew something that she did not. It was not long before Kathy placed a person with her suspicions.

To this point, Kathy had not shared any of her suspicions with Mark, but she could be silent no longer. As she and Mark drove from the party to her hotel, Kathy began to open up her heart. She talked about her love for Mark, her confusion regarding his behavior, and her concern for their marriage. Kathy also stated her suspicions regarding Nancy, one of the women she had met at the party. It was then that Kathy asked Mark if there was anything he needed to tell her. Mark may not have been much of a writer, but neither was he much of a liar. Kathy had always found him to be truthful.

Kathy's confrontation brought silence in the car. Mark continued to drive, but he did not speak. Finally, the car came to a stop. The silence continued. Mark and Kathy avoided eye contact by looking straight ahead through the windshield of the car. Several minutes passed. Finally, Mark turned toward Kathy and began to speak.

I've made some mistakes during the past few weeks. I've done some things I should not have done. I've been confused. But things are different now.

I have been involved in a special friendship, but that's over now. I'm sorry for what I've done, and I'm sorry it has hurt you. I don't want anything to come between us. I promise I will never disappoint you again.

Six months after Kathy confronted Mark regarding her suspicions, they sat in my office for their first counseling session. Since admitting to having a "special friendship," Mark had behaved in an exemplary way. He had truly invested in his marriage. But it was obvious that their relationship was in turmoil. Not much healing had taken place from the time of initial disclosure until now.

I made some stupid choices. I was wrong. I admitted that to Kathy and told her I was sorry, but it hasn't seemed to make a difference. She's still mad.

Kathy can't seem to let it go. She says she has forgiven me, but if that were the case, she'd stop bringing it up. I'm frustrated. I don't know what else she wants from me.

Mark's frustrated words were matched by an even more exasperated countenance. Throwing his hands up into the air, he collapsed back into his chair. With a deep sigh, and his arms now crossed, Mark awaited Kathy's response. He had no doubt that there would be one.

What is it that I'm supposed to forgive? You've told me nothing other than you had a "special friendship." What exactly is a special friendship? What does it mean when a married man has a special friend who is a woman?

You said you made some mistakes during those weeks in training. What mistakes? Did you hold your friend's hand? Did you kiss her? Did you sleep with her? Did you make any commitments to her?

What was going on in your head? What did you think about her? What did you think about me? What was the confusion?

Mark, you've told me nothing—nothing at all. And I need to know!

The Need to Know

There is no issue around which disagreement between offenders and their spouses is any more predictable than the issue of *disclosure*. By *disclosure*, I am referring to making known the details of the affair. Offenders and their spouses differ regarding what actually constitutes disclosure. Is it enough to simply admit to having had an affair, or does disclosure necessitate a more thorough description of participants, events, and activities?

Offenders generally hold to the belief, "The less said the better. Let's just start fresh." They would rather forget that the affair ever occurred. If they can get by with just a simple admission of guilt, they feel enough has been said. After all, "it's all in the past."

Care and concern for their marriages is frequently cited by offenders as justification for their hesitancy to disclose any more detail. They argue, "It will only cause needless pain. Some things are better left unknown. Isn't it enough to know that it happened—and that now it's over?"

Though *over*protection may truly be present, it is likely for their hesitancy to disclose information to also be *self*-protective. Discussing the specifics of an affair is embarrassing and uncomfortable and may create additional difficulties. In an offender's mind, these are three good reasons to avoid any discussion if possible.

What is the result of the tactic "the less said the better"? What does it mean for the relationship? Invariably, the result is not good. It does not satisfy the ever curious spouse. And when these failed attempts at nondisclosure produce negative results, what is an offender's response? Routinely, he makes the following accusations regarding his spouse:

"She won't let it go." (Implying that the spouse is being vindictive.)

"He can't get over it." (Implying that the spouse is emotionally unhealthy.)

"She hasn't really forgiven me." (Implying that there is something wrong with the spouse's spirituality.)

"I've admitted to the affair, but that doesn't seem to be enough. He wants more. What else can I do?" (Implying that the spouse is unreasonable and wants too much.)

As can be noted in these accusations, an offender sees it as the spouse's problem, not his own. He believes, "If she would just straighten up, everything would be fine."

On the other hand, offended spouses want to hear the facts—to know each and every detail. Simple admission of guilt is not enough. For the offended spouse, *admission does not equal disclosure.* Names, places, times, events—these are the elements that comprise disclosure. They want to know *who.* They want to know *why.* They want to know "what in the world were you thinking of?" And nothing short of complete disclosure will satisfy.

The battle line is clear: the need to keep secret versus the need to know. An offender asks, "When is enough, enough?" A spouse replies, "You haven't told me anything yet. Why do you continue to protect yourself and her?" An offender asserts, "You're harassing me!" A frustrated spouse retorts, "Give me some answers and I'll stop asking questions!" One volleys, the other counters, the battle rages. When will it end?

What do you do? Should there be disclosure? If so, are there limits to what is shared? What is the appropriate course of action? With rare exception, my position is for a complete disclosure of the details of an affair. Couples can far better withstand the *crisis* brought about by the known than they can the *void* which is created by the unknown.

I understand all of the accusations made by offenders. There may even be some truth to the behavioral components of their accusations. Some spouses "won't let it go." Others "can't get over it." But the implied motivations (vindictiveness, emotional unhealthiness, questionable spirituality, etc.) are inaccurate. The undesired behaviors of the spouses are not the result of any particular deficiency or unhealthiness on their part. They are the normal responses to nondisclosure on the part of the offenders. The only thing that is lacking is information.

A betrayed spouse will have questions—many of them. These unanswered questions serve as ghosts, haunting the marriage as a constant reminder of the past. In order for the past to be let go, it must first be faced—and this confrontation must be total and absolute.

The goal in facing the past, in asking and answering all the questions, is not to unduly belabor or punish. This point must be strongly emphasized and enforced. You face the past in order to let it go. Once you've thoroughly faced the questions and successfully let the past go, do not return to it.

I inform my clients that we're dealing with disclosure once and for all. We get it done in one session. We may address a lingering question or two at the next session, but that's it. Once there has been thorough disclosure, I do not allow the spouse to return to the subject of the affair. To do so is to obsess about the betrayal, and this only keeps a couple stuck in the pain. There is no healing until they let the affair go.

The overriding principle continues to be this: An affair has to be faced in order for it to be resolved. Answering the unanswered questions of an affair is only one of the crucial tasks that must be accomplished before a couple will be ready to begin the more long-term work of restoring their marriage, but it is a step that cannot be omitted.

What Is Fair to Ask?

Offenders become anxious when they realize that disclosure means more than admission. When they realize that the restoration process requires *complete* disclosure, they become outright frightened. "Are there no limits to what my spouse can ask? Do I have to tell her everything?"

On the opposite side of the battle are the betrayed spouses who, though needing to know, are just as anxious and frightened about what they may hear. They are so frightened that they may fail to ask some of the questions that need to be addressed for the affair to be resolved.

As a rule, I encourage spouses to come to the session with a prepared list of questions. This will help to counter the forgetfulness factor which sometimes arises in tense situations. I also serve as a referee, sometimes informing an offender that a spouse's question is legitimate and deserving of an honest response, at other times suggesting neglected questions to a spouse, and occasionally intervening when I think a particular question is inappropriate. In regard to this latter point (inappropriate questions), there isn't much that cannot be discussed. With the exception of sexually explicit details, I encourage a spouse to ask anything that concerns him or her.

To aid you as a counselor and, in this particular session, as a referee, I have prepared a list of common and legitimate questions that need to be answered regarding marital betrayal. A spouse may ask some that are not listed here, but these should be considered a bare minimum.

> With whom did you have an affair?
> How and when did you meet?
> Who pursued who in the relationship?
> Who else knew of your relationship?
> How much money did you spend on her/he spend on you?
> Where did you take her/were you taken?
> When did the relationship become sexual?
> How many times did you have sex?
> Where did you have sex?
> Did you ever have sex in our house?

Did you ever have sex in our bed?
Has the relationship been severed?
Who broke it off?
How do you feel about him/her now?
Has there ever been anyone else?
Is there anything else that I should know?

Mark and Kathy

Remember the Petersons? Remember Mark's exasperated words? "I made some stupid choices. . . . I admitted that to Kathy. . . . I don't know what else she wants from me." Remember Kathy's response? "You've told me nothing. . . . I need to know!" Remember the tension—the lack of healing in their relationship? All of this changed after full disclosure. The tension between Mark and Kathy dissolved. Healing was experienced in their relationship.

Kathy needed to know what Mark meant by *mistakes*. She needed to know what he meant by *confusion*. What had he done that was wrong—that was in need of forgiveness? What exactly was a "special friend"—and how really special was this friend? When Kathy received answers to these and other legitimate questions, she knew what needed to be forgiven. There was pain with this complete disclosure, but there was also cleansing and healing. The ghosts were gone. Mark and Kathy were freed to deal with restoration. Full disclosure enabled this couple to truly bury the past and face the future.

Quick-Scan 6

Things to remember about disclosure

✓ Disclosure—making known the details of the affair—needs to be *complete*.

✓ Challenge the overprotective and self-protective rationales which foster avoidance of disclosure.

- Admission does not equal disclosure.
- Couples can far better withstand the *crisis* brought about by the known than they can the *void* created by the unknown.
- Offended spouses need to know in order to not be haunted.

✓ Establish your role as a referee for this session.

- Define the parameters: All is fair except sexually explicit questions.
- Determine what is legitimate and what is not.
- Have a spouse come with a prepared list of questions.
- Help by asking any essential questions you believe have been omitted.
- Encourage an offender to truthfully answer all legitimate questions.

✓ Move away from the betrayal and on to the marriage.

- Once all questions are sufficiently answered, leave the aspect of the marital betrayal behind.
- Move forward to the marriage.
- Do not allow the focus to return to the betrayal.

Part 3

Blocks to Restoration—Resistance

10

"I Can't Get Past the Affair!"

I had met with Anne and Paul for several sessions. We had worked through the joining process where the therapeutic relationship was established. I had conducted individual preparatory sessions with them both. We then spent three sessions talking about the affair, working through a reconciliation process, and making sure there were no unanswered questions to act as ghosts of the betrayal. Everything had been done. Still, as I gazed upon this couple at the beginning of another session, I suspected that we had not yet turned the corner. Anne and Paul were still living with the affair. They were stuck.

My suspicion was based on a visual assessment. Let me caution that you not read too much into observable factors alone. Observations can prompt hypotheses warranting further evaluation. Once additional data is received, you are then free to make firmer conclusions. A single observation, however, should never be taken as a sole indicator of either good or bad. With this in mind, I proceeded cautiously. Still, though neither Anne nor Paul had uttered a word, their body language spoke very loudly. Anne's pensive posture (perched on the edge of her seat) and Paul's sprawled body (wilted, limp, and leaning as far away from Anne as he could possibly get) suggested an air of tension. Anne looked intense. She was a woman on a mission. Paul just looked weary. More than mere fatigue, Paul's sighs suggested exasperation and defeat.

My initial inquiry, "How are things going?" was met with silence. Neither Anne nor Paul was eager to pick up the gauntlet. I waited.

It is important that you become comfortable with silence. Do not let it control your interventions. Silence can add tension to a session—for clients and counselors. Your own personal discomfort with silence should not prompt some kind of comment that interferes with what is taking place. If you must break the silence, be certain of your motivation. Make sure your actions are based on a conscious decision to move the counseling in a particular direction and not merely to ease your own personal discomfort.

Anne and Paul's silence was deafening. After what seemed to be several minutes, I broke the silence with another comment. "Are things that bad?" This brought more silence. Anne gazed at Paul as if to ask him to respond first, but she could not catch his eye. Paul was content to stare at the floor. I chose to wait. Finally, Paul began to speak. His words were slow and deliberate.

I'm ready to give up. What's the use? Anne can't seem to get past what I did. She won't let it go. Instead, she just keeps harping on the same old thing. "How could you do it? How could you treat me this way?"

I know I did wrong. But how long are we going to dwell on this? I'm ready to move on—but I guess she isn't. (Paul paused for a moment and slowly took a deep breath.) My real fear is that it will never be any different—that Anne will always hold the affair against me, and our relationship will never be any better than it is right now. I don't think I can stand that.

Paul's words matched his body language. Tired, exasperated,

nearly hopeless—his exhortation brought both clarification and meaning to the visual picture. Then Anne responded.

Paul is right. I do harass him. I can't seem to stop. But he really hurt me!

I want to get over it. I want our marriage to be better. But I keep thinking of what he did. I didn't deserve that! He deceived me. He ruined our lives, and now he wants things to go on as if they never happened. I just don't know if I can do that.

Paul says he was wrong, but I don't know that he really believes he was wrong. When I'm upset, he just tries to lighten things up with a humorous comment. He doesn't take what he did or how I feel seriously. I don't think he's really sorry either. At least he's not sorry enough!

He's right. I can't let it go. I can't seem to get over what he did. I love him, but I continue to stay mad at him. I can't get past the affair!

Where Is the Impasse?

Anne and Paul were stuck. Neither one of them denied this fact. But where was the impasse? Was it with Paul? Was Anne correct when she accused Paul of not believing he was really wrong and of not being really sorry? That was possible. Perhaps Anne and Paul had only accomplished a sloppy reconciliation. This would have been the case if Paul had said all the right things with his lips but had not believed them in his heart. Perhaps he was the problem. On the other hand, maybe Anne was the impasse. After all, how much is enough? If Paul was as honest and genuinely remorseful as he claimed, how much more could he do? Was he correct in his exasperation: "What's the use . . . it will never be any better"?

As a counselor, your first task is to determine where the impasse lies. That decision will direct your intervention. I worked through a list of diagnostic questions. Some of the answers required my subjective evaluation. Sometimes your subjective "feel" for a situation is all you have to go on. Was Paul (the offender) failing to accept responsibility for the affair? Was Anne (the offended) failing to accept her contribution to the deterioration of the marriage? Had Paul demonstrated remorse, asked Anne's forgiveness, and committed himself to the restoration of the marriage? Had Anne accepted Paul's overtures to the marriage and extended forgiveness? Were there any particular personality characteristics limiting Anne's ability to let the affair go (i.e., was she excessively insecure)? The answers to these questions would give me direction.

As I mentally worked through my checklist of questions, it seemed that the impasse rested in Anne and not Paul. The block was not with the offender but with the offended. Anne had a *lingering obsession*. In spite of the many constructive efforts being made by Paul to move their relationship along, she could not get her focus off of the affair. Anne would have to be the focus of my attention.

Being Desperately Normal

We were stuck. Anne and Paul knew it, and so did I. For restoration to continue, something had to happen to break through the block. I was actually facing two problems. The restoration process was obviously blocked, but almost as importantly, Anne and Paul were thinking about giving up. They were each beginning to feel hopeless. Doubting that things could get any better, they felt like quitting. Somehow, I needed to address both problems—the problem of their particular variation of resistance (the lingering obsession) and the emotional residue (disillusionment) that this blockage precipitated.

When confronting an impasse, regardless of the variation, I generally approach the couple from a position that reframes their situation from one of utter hopelessness to that of being *desperately normal.* I want their cooperation in confronting the problem, so I do not minimize the seriousness of their circumstance. They must see the reality of their situation plainly so that they will do something about it. Yet I do not want to take away what little hope they have left. It would even be better if I could increase their hope a little. What follows is an example of treating a very real block to restoration as a desperately normal situation.

Well, we're stuck. As much as we need to leave the affair in the past and move on to the more important task of dealing with the marriage, you are not ready to do that.

Your marriage needs for you to move on, and I know you both wish you could. But needs and wishes don't change reality. If you're not ready, then you're not ready. The problem is this, however: Either you will resolve whatever is blocking you and let the affair go, or your marriage will end. You may decide not to divorce—to keep the institution alive—but the relationship will die. It's as simple as that. Move on or die. (Pause)

Now, I think we can get past the blockage. If things were progressing in an ideal fashion, we would have already turned the corner. But life isn't always ideal, and getting stuck isn't all that unusual. We can probably deal with this, but it's going to take your cooperation.

Anne, I'd like to meet with you for another individual session. We need to deal with your feelings regarding the affair. I know Paul hurt you, but you're bordering on an obsession with the betrayal. We need to face it and let it go.

My goal was to gain Anne and Paul's cooperation by impressing upon them the dire circumstances of their dilemma—the consequence for their marriage if they remained at the present impasse. This was accomplished by speaking of the possible death of their relationship. Though these words were heavy, a sense of optimism and hopefulness was imparted by my suggesting the normality of their situation. "Your situation is desperate but by no means impossible. In fact, it's fairly typical."

With the desperateness of their situation stressed, but also the hopefulness for change, I requested an individual session with Anne. In this particular relationship, it appeared to be Anne who was holding the marriage to the past. Anne was very willing to meet with me for an individual session; she knew she had a problem. She was clearly aware of the difficulty that her clinging to the past was creating for any hope for restoration. But more than mere understanding, Anne was also aware of the personal discomfort which accompanied her obsession. Anne was in pain, and she was ready to be rid of both the obsession and the emotional discomfort.

The Forgiveness Factor

At the core of most lingering obsessions is a feigned attempt at forgiveness. Failure to forgive usually rests in a breakdown in one of two areas. First, failure to truly forgive may be the result of personal denial and psychological rigidity on the part of the offended spouse. This is illustrated in the following attitude.

I was perfect. Our marriage was perfect. The only thing that was not perfect is what he did. How could he do that to me? I didn't deserve it. There is nothing he can ever do to make up for what he did!

This type of superiority greatly inhibits forgiveness and reflects tremendous denial on the part of the offended spouse. There needs to be a realistic acceptance of personal contribution to the prebetrayal marital condition.

A second reason for the failure to truly forgive may be related to a cursory and superficial handling of what is in reality an extremely complex and in-depth process. With the strong emphasis in the conservative Christian community to offer instantaneous absolution, it is not uncommon for quick forgiveness to result in lingering, yet deeply harbored, resentment. Working through the forgiveness process—dealing with the big hurts—can take a considerable length of time.

It takes time for an injured party to honestly face the pain—to break through the protective veneer of denial and *visualize* the wound, to *admit* the true extent of the injury, and to *express* the depth of feelings and hurt. It takes time to clearly identify the source of the wound and to express just how much pain the betrayal has inflicted. It takes time to get to the place where there is a willingness to make the cognitive *choice* to forgive. With both the pain and its source faced, the decision to choose forgiveness is an indication of readiness to face the future. As Dr. David Schell suggests in his book *Getting Bitter or Getting Better: Choosing Forgiveness for Your Own Good* (Meinrod, Ind.: Abbey Press, 1991), a choice is made to get *better* instead of *bitter*. An injured spouse does not necessarily feel better, but she wants to. Having painstakingly worked through the prerequisite steps, she is ready to make that choice.

There are several elements involved in resolving a lingering obsession. In addressing these elements, most of your counsel will be aimed at aiding an offended spouse to work through an uncompleted forgiveness. Whether forgiveness has been hindered by personal denial and psychological rigidity, the superficial handling of a complex forgiveness process, or a combination of both of these factors, the impasse is resolvable. For you to bring resolution, however, you will need to bring completeness to forgiveness.

Resolving a Lingering Obsession

The time lapse between sessions had not allowed any of Anne's tension to diminish. She still sat on the edge of her seat. But there was a change in her outlook. Anne seemed to be more accepting of the possibility that *she* had a problem. As much as she would like to have laid any setbacks at Paul's feet, she no longer could deny the reality that she had never quite forgiven him for what he had done. "I know what I'm doing. I know I haven't really forgiven Paul. But I've got to get past it."

In resolving a lingering obsession, I spend a session or two focusing on the process of forgiveness and the possibility of the presence of any personal superiority. Though there is no set sequence, I make sure that my intervention involves at least the following elements:

Expressing Feelings

Anne needed an opportunity to express her feelings—to get it all out. So I gave her permission to do so in our session. I coached Anne in identifying her pain—all of the ways she was hurt by what Paul had done. She cried as she shared about feeling abandoned and left to provide for her family on her own. Her sobs increased as she talked about the sense of rejection and the crushing blow that the affair had dealt to her self-esteem. And there was pain surrounding the humiliation that Paul's betrayal had caused for Anne among her peers. She felt ashamed to even go out in public. All of this pain was the result of what he had done.

Anne had less difficulty identifying the culprit than she did in facing the fragmented myriad of hurts. Anne knew it was Paul's inappropriate behavior that had precipitated her pain. Still, she sensed guilt as she verbalized her accusations. After all, she was supposed to turn the other cheek. She was supposed to forgive. She was supposed to forget it ever happened. To clearly say that Paul had done her wrong was foreign. I encouraged Anne to acknowledge both the legitimacy of her pain as well as the wrongness of Paul's deed.

Sometimes it is good to give clients written assignments to deal with this type of therapeutic work. I frequently assign the task of letter writing and instruct clients to spend several hours getting in touch with their feelings and creating a document (which will remain unmailed) that allows the opportunity of honest self-exploration and expression of pain. This type of activity is not an end in itself, but it is an important part of the process. Clients need to know what it is that they are going to let go of.

Clarifying Perceptions

Anne had only superficially dealt with forgiving Paul. I was making efforts to allow her to deal more honestly with her pain and the choices involved in completing the process, but there were also hints of self-righteousness and superiority in her attitude. Paul had truly betrayed both Anne and their marriage, but the marriage had not been perfect. The imperfections did not justify Paul's inappropriate behavior, but Anne's denial of any personal imperfections, and the further denial of any problems within their relationship, fostered a rigidity which interfered with her ability to forgive and move on. I needed to challenge or clarify her perceptions of their prebetrayal relationship and encourage Anne to take responsibility for what was legitimately hers to own.

Anne and I talked about marriage. We started with marriage in general—with what ought to be happening for a relationship to approach what God intended. We then began to focus on her marriage specifically—on the relationship she and Paul had before the betrayal. As I folded in some of the complaints that I had heard from Paul with some other descriptions from Anne, it became clear that their marriage had been flawed. Whether overt or covert, whether intentional or unintentional, and whether through commission or omission, their relationship had not been perfect. And contributions for this imperfection were the responsibility of both spouses—not just Paul.

Taking away a person's saintliness seems to improve their attitude toward forgiveness. It is much easier to assume the role of a forgiver when you recognize your own need to also be forgiven. My message to Anne was that there were some things that she could have done differently. There were other things that she should have been aware of. Her imperfections may not have been great, but they were there nonetheless. Still, though the history had been marred, the future could be better. "You have the opportunity to make it right. At least, you have the opportunity to take care of your part."

Anne began to own her responsibility. This resulted in a loosening of her rigidity and a lessening of her self-righteousness. A transformation seemed to be taking place.

Determining Goals

Anne needed motivation to change. She needed a reason to let go of the betrayal. Granted, dealing with forgiveness and her need to be forgiving was a strong rationale in and of itself. However, there needed to be a realization of just what failing to forgive Paul would mean for her and her marriage—what it would cost her. I approached this by dealing with her goals.

What do you want to see happen, Anne? What is your goal? Is it for marital restoration, or is it for the marriage to end?

Anne's response was predictable. She wanted their relationship to be healed. She wanted them to be whole again—to feel good about each other, to trust, and to sense a commitment to the marriage.

Well, if that's what you want to see happen for you and Paul, is what you're doing now going to help that occur? Is clinging to the past going to bring healing for your marriage? Is it going to help you reach your goal? I don't think so.
How long are you going to live in the past? How long are you going to let clinging to the betrayal frustrate your life

and i
Paul
A
conti

D
said
was
bein
her
wor
I
that
ing
was
Of
for
sity
Pau

ever, the choice to either complete the fo
to cling to the past rests with the offend
Anne had to make a choice. Was s
go? Was she ready to forgive Pau
tinue in her march toward bitt
Anne. What are you going
Anne appeared calmer
ent at the beginning o
clear whether the c
tioning of her sa
for her marri
trayal. I or

Choosing Forgiveness

Forgiveness is a choice. It is not something that an individual can be forced to do. Possibly the words can be forced but not the heart attitude. In the case of marital betrayal, an offended spouse has to be ready to offer forgiveness before it can be truly extended.

As a counselor, your role is to influence, not control. Realistically, it is questionable whether you can truly control what someone else does anyway, at least for any length of time. When it comes to your influencing a spouse who possesses a lingering obsession, you are attempting to aid her in completing the forgiveness process. You allow her to vent; you challenge her saintliness; and you apply some pressure by forcing her to look at the consequences of her present behavior. Ultimately, how-

giveness process or
ed spouse.

he ready to let the betrayal
l? Or was she going to con-
rness? "Forgiveness is a choice,
o do?"

now. The intensity that had been pres-
the session had diminished. It was un-
ange was the result of her venting, the ques-
ntliness, or the realization of the consequences
age should she continue to obsess about the be-
ly knew that something was different.

n ready to let it go. I'm ready for Paul and me to move
. I'm ready to forgive him. I know I'm supposed to, and I
know things will go better for us if I do. But I'm not doing it
for either of those reasons. It's not out of duty or bargaining.
I'm forgiving Paul because I want to.

I can't say that I won't have some momentary flashbacks,
but I'm making the choice to let the past go. I want to move
on. I feel resolved about that decision. There is a sense of
peace about this that I haven't had before. I think I'm ready
to deal with our marriage.

With Anne's statement of resolve, our session moved to closure. Paul and Anne began meeting conjointly on a regular
basis, and we were able to focus attention on their marriage.
There was plenty of work left to be done, but we had turned
the corner. With Anne's unfinished forgiveness finally completed, we were able to proceed toward the restoration of their
relationship.

Quick-Scan 7

Things to remember about a lingering obsession

✓ Determine that the impasse rests with the offended spouse's uncompleted forgiveness.

✓ Instill hope and enlist the couple's cooperation.

- Inform of normality of their situation.
- Enlist cooperation (maintain stress) by describing the desperateness of their situation if there is no change.

✓ Allow the forgiveness process to be completed.

- Allow spouse to vent—to talk about the pain.
- Enable spouse to identify the source of the pain.
- Challenge any self-righteous attitudes.
- Reaffirm the spouse's goal for marital restoration as opposed to divorce and the consequences for the relationship if forgiveness is not achieved.
- Encourage the spouse to choose to forgive.

11

"I Won't Jump through Hoops!"

"Sue just wants me to jump through hoops, and I'm tired of it!" With that statement, Peter crossed his arms and sank back into his chair. The atmosphere in the office grew cold. Peter just stared at his wife. Sue was obviously stunned by Peter's words and appeared to be grasping for exactly what to say. Should she deny Peter's accusation? Should she admit to it? Should she explain her behavior—make another attempt to gain Peter's cooperation? Her mind was racing. All the while as she diligently searched for an appropriate response, Peter sat stoically and motionless. His posture was defiant as if to say, "I've done all I am going to do. I will not be moved from this position."

By using the phrase "jump through hoops," Peter was accusing Sue of overstepping the bounds of legitimate expectations for his behavior. Was Peter correct in suggesting that Sue was demanding? Was Sue actually placing unnecessary obstacles in the way of marital restoration? Was she being vindictive and difficult? Or, contrary to Peter's beliefs, was Sue actually stating healthy and legitimate expectations? Was it in fact Peter who was being difficult? Was Peter offering unnecessary resistance? Was he being unreasonable and uncooperative? Did he fear even the appearance of Sue's exerting control over his life?

Was there more at stake here than mere compliance to a request? You be the judge.

Sue and Peter are veterans of a thirty-year marriage. It was nearly two years earlier that Sue began to suspect the possibility of another woman in Peter's life. Peter was careful to cover the tracks of his indiscretion. He had left none of the "hard signs" for Sue to discover (hotel or gift receipts; telephone charges; notes, cards, phone numbers, and messages lying around; unexplained telephone calls to the home). It was the "soft signs" that had aroused Sue's suspicions. It was the change in his routine—the unexplained and unaccounted for gaps of time in his previously normal and predictable schedule—and the inconsistencies in his stories when Sue would ask him questions that began to cause her some alarm. The soft signs may have gone unnoticed in another relationship. Some other wife may have been far less suspecting, but for Sue, the soft signs prompted a remembrance of earlier times. She had seen them all before, and she remembered what they had meant.

At first, I just fought my suspicions. I kept telling myself that, surely, it couldn't be happening again. But the subtle indicators were all there. Once I accepted the fact that it could possibly be reoccurring, I began to see even more evidence that Peter was involved with someone else.

Of course, Peter denied it. I didn't make an outright accusation. I just began to ask questions about his whereabouts. Peter knew what was going on. He quickly reacted with complaints about my not trusting him. "How long are you going to make me pay for the past?" I vacillated between feeling guilty for not trusting him to feeling angry for what I really believed he was doing.

I think I have been as angry with his blatant lying as I have with his unfaithfulness. It's one thing for Peter to be unfaithful. It's something all together different for him to lie about it and attempt to make it appear that the problem was really with me—with my being overly suspicious, nontrusting, or ba-sically insecure.

I really anguished over the guilt. Peter could be so con-vincing, so "unjustly persecuted." Had I not gotten photographs, actual proof of his secret rendezvous, I don't know to this day if he would have ever admitted the truth. I still don't know everything. Peter's pattern is to deny anything and every-thing until tangible and undeniable proof contradicts his story. Then and only then, he admits to only those things that actual hard evidence no longer allows him to deny.

Peter has never been truthful with me up front. His hon-esty has always been after the fact when he had no other re-course. With this pattern, I have to work real hard at trust-ing Peter. I have been willing to do that in the past, and I want to do it again. But this time, I need more from him.

I need to know what is going on in Peter. Why does he have this need to seek out other relationships? This is the fourth occurrence in our thirty years of marriage. There must be a problem in Peter—some reason for his behavior. We're not talking about one quick fling here. There's a pattern—a repetitive history for this type of behavior. There is obviously some deeper problem. I need to know what it is and what may be the likelihood of any future occurrence.

Peter had had three previous affairs. At least he had had three of which Sue was aware. All of these had been handled in a sim-ilar fashion. Through either careless behavior or anonymous tips, Sue would become suspicious of Peter's extramarital ac-tivities. Finally, a confrontation would take place followed by a series of vehement and indignant denials by Peter. Ultimately, factual evidence would be presented that Peter could no longer deny, and he would admit to some generalized wrongdoing (no specifics given or discussed), casually ask for Sue's forgiveness, and promise to be forever faithful. Following a brief time of restoration, the marriage would resume as if nothing had ever happened.

That had been the superficial manner in which the previous indiscretions had been handled. But this time things were different. Sue was determined to break the cycle. The discovery of this last affair prompted a separation that lasted nearly one and one-half years. Peter had not wanted Sue to move out. He wanted to deal with this instance in the same manner as all the rest, but Sue had other plans. There were prerequisites that would have to be met if they were to reconcile and continue in their marriage.

Expectations versus Demands

Sue's expectations fell into three groupings. Each prerequisite related to either the present-tense reconciliation of their relationship, Sue's personal safety, or her hope for the future-tense of their marriage. Upon separating from Peter, Sue indicated that any plans to reunite would be preceded by his completing several tasks. There would have to be a thorough discussion of the affair, including a disclosure of all pertinent details. Peter would have to make genuine statements such as, "I was wrong," "I'm sorry," and "I'm committed to this marriage." Also, Peter would have to undergo some blood tests to insure that he was not transmitting any STDs (sexually transmitted diseases), including the deadly HIV. And finally, Peter would have to seek professional help for his personal difficulty. Sue wanted Peter to see a specialist who could diagnose and treat whatever it was that compelled him to infidelity.

What do you think? Was Sue being vindictive? Was she being controlling? Was she crossing Peter's legitimate boundaries? At first, Peter was outraged with what he termed "Sue's demands." He saw them as controlling, unreasonable, and humiliating. Peter countered with a demand of his own: "Either come home or file!" Sue stood firm. She was prepared to give the separation some time, neither hastily ending the marriage nor prematurely returning home. Failing to coerce Sue into returning home with the threat of divorce, Peter tried being nice and attempted to convince Sue that the best thing for both of them would be for her to return. Again, Sue stood firm. Peter's last manipulation was with helplessness. He became desperate. "I'm really hurting, Sue. I can't go on without you."

All of these actions were attempts to get the relationship back to the way it was prior to the separation. Peter had not changed, nor did he intend to. But Sue stood firm. There would have to be more than superficial handling for her to reunite with Peter. The marriage would have to be different. For there to be any possibility for their relationship to be different, Sue's expectations would have to be met.

Gradually, Peter began to concede. There were several months where no progress was made at all. In fact, communication all but ceased. Then Peter began to accept and adapt to the new standard that had been set by Sue. One by one, though with reluctance each time, Peter met all of Sue's stated expectations. All, that is, except for seeing a specialist for treatment. To this, he refused. This expectation is what prompted the introductory statement for this chapter: "Sue just wants me to jump through hoops. . . ."

Every time I give in and meet one of her demands, she adds something else to her list. I'm beginning to think that she doesn't really want me back after all. Sue's only interest is in getting back at me for what I did to her. She just wants me to jump through hoops.

Here was the impasse. What Sue identified as an expectation for restoration, Peter viewed as a demand. What Sue termed legitimate, Peter decried as illegitimate. Who was right? Who was being unreasonable? Who would have to concede? What do you think? Upon what is your decision based?

Is It Reasonable?

In dealing with an impasse of this nature, there are really two questions which need to be answered. The first question addresses the issue of appropriateness: What is *reasonable* to expect? This may require a judgment call on your part. It's not necessarily your role to take sides in a marital disagreement (though there are times when you will lean to one side or the other). Neither is it your goal to do so in this instance. However, identifying what is healthy and encouraging a couple to move in that direction automatically places you in a directive position.

When it comes to expectations, what is reasonable? The rule of thumb is this: *What is helpful for health, healing, and growth within the relationship is appropriate.* Though each couple may present some characteristics that are unique to them, generic expectations fall in the three categories illustrated by Sue's prerequisites for Peter: (1) present-tense reconciliation of the relationship, (2) upholding personal safety, and (3) restoring hope for the future-tense of the marriage.

Present-Tense Reconciliation of the Relationship

Is it reasonable for a betrayed spouse to expect to discuss the affair—even to vent his or her pain? Or is this too much to ask? Some would argue that discussions of this type are negative and border on vindictive and harassing behavior. If carried to excess, this could be true. Within acceptable limits, however, I see this as a healthy prerequisite to healing and restoration.

Having read the earlier portions of this book, you should be able to determine other reasonable expectations for this category. Is it reasonable to expect full disclosure of the details of an affair? Certainly. Though an offender may feel discomfort with disclosure, it is clearly a reasonable (and necessary) expectation. Is it reasonable to expect admission of wrongdoing, statements of sorrow and remorse, and requests for forgiveness? Certainly. Though an offender may prefer to just forget the affair ever happened, without these types of interchanges, there is no reconciliation. The question is, What is reasonable? The answer is found in meeting the following criteria: Is it healthy, healing, and growth producing?

Upholding Personal Safety

The most important personal safety concerns apply to either protection from infectious diseases or protection from abusive behavior. Is it legitimate to expect personal safety within a relationship? Certainly. How does this legitimate expectation convert to specifics within a marriage?

Regarding a concern for infectious diseases, Sue's requirement that Peter undergo a thorough medical evaluation, including blood tests, seemed appropriate. He attacked the idea citing the discomfort of personal humiliation and Sue's vindictive nature as reasons for noncompliance. Though reluctant, Peter ultimately submitted to the tests. Was Sue being unreasonable? Based on the fact that Peter had been sexually involved with another person, requiring a medical clean bill of health was both wise and prudent.

Dealing with abusive behavior is not as simple to resolve. Where there has been a history of abusiveness, either through threat, intimidation, demeaning language, or actual physical assault, the rule of thumb is for there to be demonstrated behavioral change over time. It is reasonable to expect more than the promise of safety. Changed behavior must be demonstrated over a significant period of time.

Restoring Hope for the Future-Tense of the Marriage

Not every relationship will have expectations in this category. When present, these usually include the involvement of some form of professional treatment. Again, Sue and Peter serve as an example. The repetitive history of Peter's unfaithfulness suggested the probability of a deep problem—something beyond simple marital dissatisfaction. Though he may do all the right things to reconcile his marriage, if nothing is changed inside Peter, what is the likelihood that the problem of infidelity would resurface at a later time?

This was the dilemma that Sue faced. It was Peter's history (the repetitive pattern of behavior) and not the incident of unfaithfulness in and of itself which prompted Sue to expect an in-depth professional evaluation. She needed a reason to believe the future would be different than the past.

It is legitimate to expect professional involvement when there is a history of inappropriate behavior as opposed to a single episode or event. Hope does not leave a marriage because of an incident; it departs due to repetitive acts—it is methodically beaten out of a relationship. For hope to return, something tangible must occur. A betrayed spouse has to have a reason to believe that things can be different. The offender's positive experience in therapy can give a disillusioned spouse a reason to have hope.

In the situation illustrated by Sue and Peter, especially in view of their personal history, I did not see anything unreasonable in Sue's expectations. The unreasonable behavior seemed to be with Peter's reluctance to cooperate with Sue and the manner in which he still tried to manipulate the situation. He was making statements that were totally false in an effort to gain concessions. First, in an effort to cast Sue in the light of being an unreasonable person, he termed her expectations as demands. He made this clearer when he accused Sue of being vindictive, claiming that her only goal was in punishing and humiliating him and not in bringing restoration to their marriage. Second, Peter stated that Sue kept adding more demands to her list. This was false. There was nothing on Sue's list at our counseling session that had not been clearly stated at the outset of their separation.

Based on an examination of the facts of their situation, it was easy to answer the question, What is reasonable? Sue's requests were more than appropriate. They encouraged health, healing, and marital growth. In facing this particular impasse, however, a second question must also be answered. It is not enough to determine the presence of appropriateness alone, the issue of *motivation* must also be faced. This prompts our second question. If the spouse's prerequisites are reasonable expectations, why is the offender so reluctant to cooperate? What is the *real* problem?

What Is the *Real* Problem?

If there is no legitimacy in the offender's accusations—if the offended spouse's expectations are reasonable—then the offender's motivation must be illegitimate. If the offended spouse is not being vindictive or rigid, then what is the *true* motivation of the offender? What is the *real* problem? Why the resistance?

Describing requests as demands, viewing legitimate expectations as unreasonable hoops to be jumped through, defiantly stating an unwillingness to cooperate when cooperation appears called for—these characteristics suggest the presence of either (1) a resentful attitude toward the offended spouse, or (2) a personality characteristic that resists any perceived attempt of control. This latter possibility represents a more significant (deeper core issue) problem than mere resentment and extends beyond the scope of present-tense relationship difficulty. Resentment as an impasse to restoration will be addressed later (see chap. 13). The issue of control, however, is the focus of this chapter.

The discriminating factor for determining whether a control issue exists is found in the history of the marriage. A control issue leaves a trail that can be traced from the present back to the beginning of the relationship. A marital partner who refuses to jump through hoops out of an unnecessary fear of being controlled has always refused to jump through them. An alert spouse will have numerous examples to parallel the present accusations.

There's nothing new in what Peter is saying. I've heard it all before. He's always been overly sensitive to even the appearance of my trying to tell him what to do.

During our marriage, I've heard "jump through hoops" so many times that I've learned to despise the words. Peter's called me names, made accusations about my motives, even asked me if I was trying to be his mother. So, this isn't new. Just more of the same.

What has been the relational history of the marriage? Has resistance to perceived attempts at control been a problem throughout the relationship? If so, then the likelihood of a personality characteristic as opposed to a purely situational problem is high. Resolving a personality related difficulty, based on the nature and scope of the problem, can present more of a challenge than dealing with an artifact of the relationship. Impasses presented by an uncompleted forgiveness or an interrupted grief process have greater predictability. Still, if reconstruction is to proceed, the control issue must be faced.

Resolving a Control Issue

It is best if you view control issues as having two levels of intervention. The first level is superficial in nature. It focuses on the immediacy of the situation. It requires limited change (being immediately reasonable), an awareness of and admission to the presence of a deeper problem, and a commitment to dealing with the core issue (even if at a later time). The second level is more in-depth. It represents an actual therapeutic addressing of the core personality issues from which the need to either control and/or resist the appearance of control emanates. This is usually tied to significant personal issues.

In continuing with Peter and Sue as an illustration, the first level of intervention would be achieved if Peter were to cooperate with Sue's request for him to enter therapy for his pattern of infidelity. This would be a limited change on Peter's part. The core issue of control may still be present, but he would at least be demonstrating immediate reasonability. Further first-level resolution would be demonstrated by Peter's admission to a control issue problem and indication of a willingness to participate in a therapeutic process to address this personal difficulty. (Depending on the severity of the problem, treatment may run simultaneous to anything being done restoratively for the marriage.) The second level of intervention would be achieved by Peter's actual successful participation in a therapeutic process focusing on his issues pertaining to control.

The reason for viewing control issues in this bi-level paradigm is to clarify your plan of action. During this phase of marital reconciliation, success at the first level would be acceptable. For the long-term restoration of the marriage to be achieved, a second-level resolution would be necessary. However, to turn the corner on the betrayal—to get past the crisis nature of the marriage—resolving the present impasse at this superficial level is sufficient. This then dictates your immediate goals for intervention. You want to address the control issue at its first level and leave the second more in-depth core problem for either a later time or another therapist.

The goal of a level-one intervention is to gain cooperation regarding an immediate issue, awareness of and admission to the presence of a deeper problem, and a commitment to dealing with the core issue at a later time. This usually requires confrontation on the part of the counselor. A spouse who possesses a control issue (fear of being controlled) is usually oblivious to this fact. Though it may be quite apparent to others, the reality is hidden from his perception. He lives in a world of denial. "What? Me oversensitive? That's crazy! Sue's just trying to run my life!" To achieve a successful level-one intervention, the offender's delusional system will have to be challenged. This will require confrontation.

The best way to confront denial is through the presentation of facts. "This is what you're saying, but these are the facts—this is what's real. Now, how do you account for the discrepancy?" That is the approach I undertook with Peter. I met with him for an individual session in order to address the impasse in specifics. After several minutes of dialogue, I confronted Peter with the facts.

Peter, I care about you, and I care about Sue, and I care about what happens to your marriage. But quite frankly, I am very concerned about the future of this relationship. You and Sue are at an impasse. Unless this gets resolved, I really question whether we can go much further.

I've watched how you and Sue have interacted, and I've listened to your complaints—how she's demanding and controlling and just wanting you to jump through hoops. But I don't see it that way. The only one being unreasonable here is you. There is nothing that Sue is asking for that is out of line, and there's nothing that she expects today that wasn't stated at the beginning of the separation. You've totally abused the facts. I have to ask myself, "Where's the problem?"

Peter, you've got a control problem. You're hypersensitive to people telling you what to do—or at least to your perception of people telling you what to do. I don't know where you picked this up. You probably acquired it in your family while you were growing up. That's where we pick up a lot of our interactional tendencies. But where you got it isn't as important right now as whether you're going to let it continue to dictate your life.

This control issue has been a predominant theme throughout your entire marriage, and it is blocking your chances at restoration right now. This isn't an issue over whether you see a therapist or not; it's a matter of control. You've taken it personally, and that has been your pattern. Look at your life! Now you can reject what I'm saying—you can say I'm *crazy; you can say I'm just taking Sue's side; you can continue to believe the lies you've been telling yourself for years—and you can watch your marriage go right down the tubes. Or, you can accept the facts, choose to deal with your life, and possibly hold this marriage together.*

The choice is up to you, Peter. You can either continue to live in denial, or you can accept reality. Whichever you choose, however, will have definite consequences for your marriage. What's it going to be?

Peter sat silently for a few moments. There were no flashes of light in the office or tremendous facial expressions to indicate that a significant ah-ha experience had taken place for Peter. Yet as we continued to talk, it became apparent that there had been a change. The shell that had served as protection for so many years was beginning to give way. Peter didn't know why he was the way he was or exactly what could be done in order to change it, but he was at least admitting to having a problem and to the need to somehow deal with it.

We were able to resolve the control issue at this initial level, and Peter later sought help from another therapist for a deeper look at his problem. Confrontation—a statement of facts challenging the delusion under which he had been living—seemed to achieve its purpose in this case. It will not always do so. Still, it seems to be the best tactic. Remember two things as you attempt to intervene with level-one control issues. First, you *earn* the right to confront. If you have not adequately joined with your client, this type of intervention may be doomed from the start. He has to sense that you care for him and that you can be trusted. Second, be aware of your boundaries as a counselor. Do not take on too much responsibility. You can influence, but you cannot control. You can do what you know to do, but you are not responsible for the outcome. Some people are simply not willing to give up the tendencies that defeat their lives.

Quick-Scan 8

Things to remember about control issues

✓ Determine that the impasse rests not with an offended spouse's unreasonable demands but with an offender's reluctance to be cooperative.

✓ Identify the spouse's expectation(s) as reasonable and appropriate.

- It is healthy, healing, and growth producing.
- It aids present-tense reconciliation of the relationship.
- It upholds personal safety.
- It helps to restore hope for the future-tense of the marriage.

✓ Determine what the offender's resistance is related to.

- Resentment
- A need to control

✓ Evaluate the history of the marriage, searching for a control-issue pattern.

✓ Expect a level-one change as a minimum (resolution of the immediate issue). This will require confrontation of an offender's denial system with facts.

12

"I Was Wrong—but Not Really"

I believe the overriding theme of Scripture is the desire for reconciliation. Throughout the Old Testament, there are numerous examples of God's reaching out to his straying people in an attempt to bring them back into relationship with him. The New Testament tells of God's ultimate extension of grace and the utmost attempt for reconciliation—the sacrifice of his son, Jesus, for the sin of mankind. The Father sent a Savior.

With such a preponderance of this theme, there are many examples upon which to draw that illustrate the various nuances of the act of reconciliation. We have already discussed the passage in Luke 15, which is commonly referred to as "the prodigal son." This passage clearly articulates the two different roles required for reconciliation to be accomplished.

1. There must be a *forgiver*—someone who has been wronged, who is aware of the pain that has been inflicted upon him by another and yet is also willing to count it for naught, to forgive the trespass, and to embrace the one who has done wrong.

2. There must also be *one who seeks forgiveness*—someone who has done wrong and recognizes his wrongdoing, is aware of the pain that he has inflicted upon another, and

with the awareness of his wrongdoing, senses genuine remorse for the pain he has caused. Upon the realization of his sin (I was wrong) and with the brokenness and remorse which accompanies this realization (I am sorry), he seeks forgiveness from the offended party.

Reconciliation requires that both roles be played out. The offended person who chooses to forgive can find inner healing without the cooperation of the offender. Likewise, the offender who comes to himself can find inner healing without the cooperation of the offended person. However, *for a relationship to be healed—for there to be true reconciliation—there must be both a forgiver and one who seeks forgiveness.*

There is a second passage of Scripture which not only brings more clarity to the whole issue of reconciliation but also sheds some light on one of the more common blocks to reconciliation in marriages where there has been betrayal.

Luke 7:36–48 tells of Jesus' being invited to a meal in the home of Simon the Pharisee. While he was there, a woman who had obviously been touched by his life, came to see the Master. In this passage, Jesus compared and contrasted the treatment he received from Simon the Pharisee and this sinful woman. It should be noted that, though the woman's past had been immoral, her present was obviously one of forgiveness. She sought out the Master to show him her love and gratitude. Jesus contrasts the love that she displayed with that displayed by Simon, and also the level of forgiveness received by each.

Undoubtedly, there is a difference between the lives of these two principal characters. The life of the woman, reportedly one of great immorality, could be sharply contrasted with that of Simon, a Pharisee. Yet I think we oversimplify the significance of this passage if we limit its application to solely the amount of obvious sin in a person's life. Regardless of the different *quantitative* amount of our sin, the *qualitative* depth of our sinfulness is the same. The love expressed by a Pharisee can be as great as that expressed by a harlot. All that is required is for him to recognize the depth of his need and to experience the grace of God.

As Jesus told the story of the two debtors (vv. 41–43), Simon would have undoubtedly identified with the debtor who owed only fifty pieces of silver (or with someone who had no debt at all). In his mind, it clearly would have been the immoral woman who owed five hundred. But would this have been a truly accurate assessment on his part?

I suggest that this passage could represent not only the quantity of sin that exists in a person's life but could also be a picture of the actual amount of sin that is offered up for forgiveness (whether that amount be little or much, and whether that amount be part or all). Simon may not have had as much overt sin in his life compared to that of this immoral woman, but maybe he did. One thing is certain, his perception of his need (or lack of need) stood between him and the Master. His self-righteousness and indignant attitude blocked his relationship with Jesus.

Sometimes one fails to receive forgiveness not because there is no sin to be forgiven, but *because there is no sin recognized.* That was the case with Simon. He really did not see a need for any forgiveness from Jesus. After all, from Simon's vantage point, there was no sin in his life. Actually, Simon had as great a need for forgiveness as did the woman. He simply failed to recognize this fact.

At other times sin is recognized, but the true *depth* of the problem is not. It is seen, but it is discounted and transformed into something less than it truly is.

I have seen this transformation and discounting of sin take place through several different tactics. One of the more common approaches is viewing sin in light of another's behavior. The argument follows one of two lines of reasoning. Either, "My need is shallow in comparison to that of another person," or, "My sin is the result of (caused by) what he/she did." In the mind of the offender, there is little need for forgiveness because there is little in need of forgiveness. Compared to what someone else did, what he did is not so bad. Or because of what someone else did, his behavior is justified. The ultimate result of this insidious and deceptive line of reasoning is noted in our Scripture passage: "Where little has been forgiven, little love is shown" (Luke 7:47).

To be forgiven greatly necessitates a clear recognition and acceptance of your *total* sin, not just a part. The fact that the need exists is inconsequential. The need has to be recognized. I believe Simon had indebtedness equal to five hundred pieces of silver, but I doubt that he would have agreed. This failure on Simon's part resulted in both a lack of love and a lack in reconciliation.

The failure to recognize or accept the depth of your sin represents a fine point in the process of reconciliation. It has particular bearing in the restoration of marriages where there has been betrayal. Remember, reconciliation requires a forgiver and one who seeks forgiveness. But what happens when a person has a debt of five hundred pieces of silver but only recognizes fifty pieces of indebtedness? How does this impact the reconciliation process? Does it aid restoration, or does it inhibit the healing that must take place? It has been my experience that this kind of failure greatly interferes with the progress of couples intent on restoring their marriage.

When present, this problem is demonstrated by the offending spouse. It acts as a block to marital restoration. I refer to this particular block, the failure to own the totality of one's sin, as *lingering justification.* Failing to resolve this resistance can have far-reaching implications for the marriage.

Assessing the Impasse

Lingering justification is best illustrated by the statement, "I was wrong . . . but not really." Seldom are these words blatantly stated in the context of the counseling session. At least, caution seems to be exercised when both spouses are present. A justified spouse may move close to this statement when in session alone with a counselor, but the indications of justification will likely come from factors other than clear verbal admission. You will need to watch for subtle indicators. There are three such indicators that warrant attention.

1. Are you hearing too many buts? You may be hearing all of the right words: "I was wrong," and "I'm sorry." But you will find that the speaker just isn't very convincing. You discover the word *but* liberally sprinkled throughout the conversation. He may admit that it was wrong to have an affair, *but*. . . . Whenever you start hearing *buts* in the statements, it is more likely the offender believes everything that follows this conjunction rather than what precedes it.

- "I was wrong for having an affair, *but* Jill should have been a better wife."
- "I was wrong for having an affair, *but* Tom and I had been drifting apart for years."
- "I was wrong for having an affair, *but* hitting forty made me crazy."

All of these statements could be true. Jill possibly could have been a better wife. The second couple may have drifted apart. The last spouse might have had a difficult time with midlife crisis. Our problem does not come with the indication of reality but with the assignment of responsibility. It is always good to understand how and why things happen, but these phrases suggest more than understanding alone. There is the implication that the responsibility for the consequential behavior rests with someone or something other than the person who actually committed the act. There is the attitude of *justification.*

- "I did it but it really wasn't my fault. Therefore, I was somewhat justified in what I did."

2. Is there an acceptance of responsibility for the wrongdoing, or does the offender dodge responsibility? Another subtle indicator is the offender's general attitude. Eventually, a justified spouse's true countenance will begin to show through. In spite of what he may be saying, an air of "What's the big deal anyway?" will begin to emerge through his facade. A justified spouse may state, "I was wrong," but you will begin to question his sincerity.

When we begin to assess subtle attitudinal cues, we move from an arena which relies solely upon objective observance of clear and concise behavior to one that relies more upon subjective and intuitive feelings. Though attitudes usually are reflected behaviorally, these signs are often masked. You may watch for hesitancies, nonchalance, flippant remarks, attempts to make light of a serious concern, etc., but much of what constitutes the behavioral characteristics of this attitude will be soft signs rather than hard signs. Ultimately, you will have to trust your instinct.

Understand this about the core belief of a justified spouse: He still fails to own his contribution to the failure of his marriage. He still believes that there are justifiable reasons for his irresponsible behavior. He is not convinced of the depth of his sin.

3. Is there appropriate remorse, or does the offender appear unmoved by the consequences of his actions? A justified spouse may say the words, "I'm sorry," but he doesn't truly feel sorrow for his actions. There is no true remorse, no true brokenness, no true recognition of the pain caused by his behavior, to either his spouse or his marriage.

Remorse is more than words and involves far more than cognitive assent. Cognitive assent is an essential part of remorse. There has to be a recognition of what has been done and a realization of what this behavior has done to others. But beyond the purely cognitive is the emotional component. Remorse is a deeply emotional entity. Scriptural examples of remorse depict a brokenness of spirit and a deep sorrow.

The lack of this emotional component, an element integrally intertwined with genuine remorse, is very noticeable. If you are hearing the right words, but emotion is absent, this should be a subtle indicator that the offender may be perpetrating a fraud. This may be a soft sign, but it is well worth investigation.

Why is there an absence of remorse? The justified spouse still fails to see the badness in what he did. His attitude is, "Especially when you consider all of the circumstances, surely, what I did was understandable." It is hard to feel remorse for doing something that was permissible to do or, at the very least, for doing something that was not terrible to do, based on all the intervening factors. "My behavior was justified."

Resolving a Lingering Justification

The reconciliation process requires two people, each portraying a distinctly different role. There must be a forgiver, and there must be one seeking forgiveness. From time to time, spouses may have to take turns, humbly exchanging their respective roles. Whichever role is taken, however, it must be embraced wholeheartedly. Being middle-of-the-road in seeking forgiveness will not bring true reconciliation.

The justified spouse is lukewarm. Sure, he admits to doing something that he should not have done, but he has an explanation—an excuse. He reasons that it was someone or something else's fault. A justified spouse admits to the behavior but not to the responsibility for his actions.

Besides being a poor line of reasoning, lingering justification blocks the restoration of a marriage. It must be challenged. When you suspect that this is the culprit, I suggest you make a general announcement to the couple that the process appears to be blocked. Utilizing a "desperately normal" reframing rationale, then ask the offender to meet with you for a private session. On an individual basis, you will challenge the offender's resistance.

You cannot make someone feel genuine remorse; this will have to come on its own. However, you can appeal to reason. An offender's sense of justification is being supported by specific thoughts. Your goal is to challenge the line of thinking that is maintaining the justified attitude—to poke holes in the delusional system. If you are successful, this block may be removed, thus allowing the restoration process to continue.

Just as each offender and each marriage is unique unto itself, each challenge to a justified attitude will be unique. Even though the specifics may vary, however, there is a common structure that can be followed for confronting most of these situations.

1. Tell the offender what you think. By this point in the process, you should have established a fairly good relationship with your client. You have to earn the right to confront. If you haven't earned the right by now, you probably aren't going to. At any rate, you have nothing to lose. Being honest and direct is your best approach.

State your concerns. Tell your client why you suggested a private meeting. Tell him what you think.

John, like I told you and Jill in our last session, I think we are stuck. We seem to have stalled, and I think at least part of the problem rests with you. I may be wrong, but I don't think so.

I've watched you and Jill over the past several weeks and one thing that strikes me is your attitude. I know you say that you were wrong to have had the affair, but I don't know if you really mean it. I question your sincerity.

I don't doubt that you regret having done it—that you see it as a mistake. But I think that you still place some of the blame with Jill for the affair occurring. If she'd only been more of what she should have been, you wouldn't have looked else-where.

Now, isn't that what you really think? Aren't you still plac-ing most of the blame for what happened on her failure in the marriage?

Some spouses will openly admit that you are correct in your assumptions. That is the easiest response for you to deal with. Others will deny your accusation. Maybe they are right and you are wrong. If they are able to convince you of your error, maybe you should stop and consider an alternative block. Possibly the spouse will have some suggestions. However, if you are not con-vinced of your inaccuracy, proceed as if the spouse were in total agreement.

It will help if you are able to state facts. Identify the specific things that warrant your suspicion of a justified attitude. I learned long ago that what people say to be true and what is ac-tually true are not always the same thing. The best way to chal-lenge this discrepancy is to state facts.

You may say this is true. You may even believe it. But whether you are trying to fool others or are only fooling your-self, the facts do not support what you are saying.

2. Challenge the rationales supporting the justification. Some-where in the rationale supporting your client's attitude of jus-tification is the belief that, because of what someone else did or did not do (or because of what did or did not happen), it was okay for him to do what he did. He may not readily admit to this belief, but his behavior is evidence enough. This belief must be challenged.

Legitimate thinking endorses the belief that "there is no *right* reason for doing the *wrong* thing." No matter what circum-stances were acting upon his life and marriage, regardless of what his wife did or did not do, nothing justifies wrong behavior. We can gain understanding of why and how people do what they do, but understanding is not license.

He messed up! He can't blame anyone else for his behavior. It was no one else's fault. Things may not have been to his liking. They may not have been of his choosing, but he still chose to do what he did. Until he grows up and accepts that responsibility—with no excuses—his behavior remains adolescent.

Your knowledge of the marriage will prove helpful at this juncture. Not only do you need to challenge the tendency to sidestep responsibility for his behavior, you also need to challenge his view of the marital failure. If the marriage deteriorated to the point where one of the spouses would seek an illicit relationship, it did so with the aid of two spouses and not just one. What were his contributions to the failure? He may readily identify the lacks in his spouse, but what were *his* errors?

Do not let him be content to place the failure totally on someone else. Here again, he needs to be confronted with the facts. It is with the acceptance of reality that the air of justification dissipates.

3. Inform the justified spouse of what needs to happen. Your role here is to simply be an educator. Share with the offender the need for reconciliation. Explain how it is only through reconciliation that healing occurs for a relationship. Inform him of the two roles required for reconciliation to take place and how each role must be genuinely played out. Then explain how his justified attitude prevents all of this from occurring.

You cannot control the behavior of people; neither would you want to. Control is not the issue here. You know what needs to happen, and you know what would definitely be in the best interest of the relationship. However, the choice of what will actually be done rests with the individuals involved.

Where there is no control, neither is there any responsibility. You may be able to influence the decisions, but do not become overly responsible for the choices that are made. By informing the justified spouse of what needs to happen, you are treating him as an adult. Based on the information that he has, he is being allowed to make decisions for which he will be responsible.

4. Predict what will be the likely outcome for his marriage if he continues to be justified. Based on everything that we know about the need for reconciliation and the factors which allow for it to happen, it does not take a rocket scientist to predict the outcome of a relationship where one spouse only flippantly admits to wrongdoing. There will not be true reconciliation; consequently, there will not be true restoration. Distance will be maintained between the spouses. Even if the relationship remains intact, it will not be intimate.

What kind of outcome does the offender desire for his marriage? What kind of relationship does he want to be a part of? His choices regarding whether he owns his responsibility or continues to reject it will greatly determine the outcome of his marriage. Again, the responsibility is his.

Final Thoughts

There is joy in reconciliation. There is joy in receiving full forgiveness. However, this is a joy that comes only to those who realize, accept, and admit to the *full* depth of their sin. Not a sin in comparison to someone else; not a sin that is the result of someone else's behavior; not a sin that can be explained by mitigating circumstances; but a sin that is fully embraced—a sin that is equivalent to a debt of five hundred pieces of silver and not just fifty.

There is joy in true remorse, not in emotionless words but true brokenness. There is joy in the sorrow that accompanies the realization of the pain that sin has inflicted on another. There is joy in having regrets.

Contrast the joy of reconciliation with the consequences of justification. The woman who washed Jesus' feet with her tears had great love. There was joy in her heart because she had been forgiven much. She reaped the benefits of her forgiveness—joy. The Pharisee also reaped the benefits of his forgiveness. However, being self-righteous—in his own perception being far less of a debtor, being justified—he was forgiven little. He reaped the benefits, but "where little has been forgiven, little love is shown" (Luke 7:47).

There was no joy in the life of the Pharisee. There was righteousness, but there was no joy. There will be no joy in the life of a justified spouse. Until he recognizes the full depth of his own sin—which is in no way meant to discount whatever sins were in the lives of others—he will be blocked in the pursuit of reconciliation. Without genuine reconciliation, there will be no healing for the marriage.

Quick-Scan 9

Things to remember about a justified attitude

✓ Determine that the impasse rests with the offender's tendency to find excuses for his behavior rather than assuming appropriate responsibility.

- Though hearing a lot of the correct words, are too many *but*s being stated by the offender?
- Is there an acceptance of responsibility for the wrong-doing?
- Is there appropriate remorse, or does the offender appear unmoved by the consequences of his actions?

✓ A justified spouse admits to the behavior but not to the responsibility for his actions.

✓ Resolving a lingering justification involves several steps.

- Announce to the couple that progress is being blocked.
- Ask to meet with the offender alone.
- Tell the offender what you think.
- Challenge the rationales supporting the justification.
- Inform the justified spouse of what needs to happen (genuine reconciliation).
- Predict the likely outcome if he continues to be justified.

13

"But I Was Hurt Too!"

In chapter 10, "I Can't Get Past the Affair!" I identified the block to marital restoration that comes from an uncompleted forgiveness process on the part of the *offended* spouse—bitterness on the part of the one who was betrayed. This type of problem does not surprise us. After all, a hurtful thing has occurred. A spouse has been rejected, a marriage violated, a sacred vow broken. The potential for bitterness is obvious. As we will now discover, those spouses who are betrayed are not the only ones in these marriages who can face the problem of bitterness and resentment. Sometimes offenders also get stuck in the mire of unforgiveness. When they do, all progress in marital restoration comes to a grinding halt.

Most of the cases where this problem is evident are characterized by emotional intensity. There is nothing light or lighthearted about bitterness. Some spouses are more outspoken than others regarding their resentment. Some prefer to explode with verbal barrages of rage while others just sullenly sulk, but their choice of expression does not change the tenor or tone of their emotion. Whether verbally explosive or quietly sullen, their intensely bitter attitude permeates the counseling environment.

I remember one couple with whom I counseled. Allen scheduled an appointment and came to my office alone for the first session. Occasionally spouses wish to begin the counseling process individually in order to present their uninterrupted perspective of the problem before having to actually deal with each other. But Allen was uncertain whether he was even willing to entertain the thought of a conjoint effort.

I believe my marriage is over. At least, that's what Cindy has told me, and I'm inclined to agree with her. I don't know that she's willing to come in for a session. But even if she is, I don't know that I really want her to.

Cindy is pretty upset with me right now. She learned of my affair. It's been over for a couple of years, but she just found out about it a month ago. It was really stupid on my part to do what I did. I know that now. It was wrong. But I don't think that's our real problem anyway.

Allen was a successful businessman, and to this point in our conversation, he had projected a calm and collected composure. However, as he began to talk about his marriage, and more specifically as he began to describe Cindy, his entire countenance went through an obvious transformation. He began to anguish. Allen's complexion flushed. His hands tightly gripped the arms of his chair. Perspiration began to appear on his brow.

We've had problems since the beginning. We can't sit down and rationally resolve anything. Cindy gets too angry. And we disagree on everything—kids, sex, money. It makes no difference what the topic is. We can disagree on it.

Cindy has always wanted more from me than I've been able to give. I find her to be abrasive and rejecting. She's so emotional. It's hard to move toward someone who yells at you. I just can't do it!

Her whole tone is marked with intensity. I need calmness—for things to be easy and quiet. She's not that way. I've fought this thing for years. I know she hasn't been happy with our marriage. I've wanted things to be different too. But I don't see how they can. Cindy is mad about the affair—but I'm mad about our life! We're just not suited for each other.

Allen was a physical wreck by the end of our session. I eventually saw Cindy and Allen conjointly, and we faced the affair. However, the real blockage for restoration came not from the betrayal. Neither did it come from Cindy. Though resistant at first, she eventually mellowed and was willing to work toward restoration. The real blockage was Allen. It centered on his resentment toward Cindy for her years of rejection. In reality, things had not been totally as Allen perceived them. Cindy was not as abrasive or rejecting as Allen had presented, but his perception served as his reality.

Allen became so angry during our sessions that he would break into tears and could not speak. He was an emotional volcano. Though his surface appearance was calm, a deeply rooted resentment smoldered just out of sight, constantly threatening to erupt, and this resentment blocked our progress.

Do Not Be Confused

It is easy to confuse the problem of unforgiveness on the part of an offender with the blockage that comes from feeling justified. Remember the justified spouse? He has excuses for his behavior. Either the affair wasn't really that significant an event, or it was actually someone else's fault. The justified spouse believes, "If only she had been a better wife," or, "If only my husband had cared more," then the affair would not have occurred. Though the problems of unforgiveness and justification may sometimes be confused, they are actually quite different in nature.

A justified spouse does not truly believe that he did anything wrong. Even if his behavior was wrong, he believes it was warranted or caused by the particular circumstances of his marital situation. Contrary to the attitude of justification, an offender caught in the throes of unforgiveness will openly admit that he was wrong. He both admits and believes that he should not have done what he did. This was illustrated in the case of Allen and Cindy. At no time did Allen blame Cindy for his behavior. In fact, he identified his actions as stupid. His exact words were: "It was really stupid on my part to do what I did. I know that now. It was wrong."

Just as in the case with Allen, an unforgiving spouse does not place the responsibility for his actions on anyone but himself. However, though there is no attempt to dodge personal responsibility, there exists a lingering and harbored feeling of disdain toward the spouse he betrayed. It is this bitterness which forms the core of his resistance to change, and it is this bitterness which must be challenged.

A Historical Problem

A resentment problem for an offender always has a historical nature. Unlike the forgiveness problem for the offended spouse, which relates specifically to the recent incident of marital betrayal, the resentment found in the offender pertains to the marriage itself. This, too, was illustrated by Allen and Cindy: "We've had problems since the beginning. . . . I've fought this thing for years." It was not one incident that created Allen's deep-seated resentment toward Cindy. It was his perception of a repetitive problem—a history—which gradually but firmly etched into Allen's soul a bitterness that threatened to consume him.

Allen's emotions were complex. He was angry with Cindy and she with him, but it was not a simple and uncomplicated anger that blocked our progress. It was resentment. There is a significant difference between the two.

I define resentment as "anger with a history." Anger is a natural human emotion. There is nothing any more inherently wrong with this emotion than there is with any of the other responses which we are created to experience. We might prefer some over others. For example, I would rather be happy than sad, but both are natural and appropriate depending upon the circumstances with which I am confronted. Resentment, on the other hand, is unhealthy. It is a mutation—a malignancy that is errantly developed through the mishandling of anger.

Scriptural concern for this potential problem is noted in Paul's letter to the Ephesians. "If you are angry, do not let anger lead you into sin; do not let sunset find you still nursing it; leave no loop-hole for the devil" (Eph. 4:26–27). Paul was indicating that a person can be angry without being in sin. His concern was that this anger not be inappropriately handled—do not nurse it. When anger is mishandled, it often leads to sin. Jesus cites the same concern in his Sermon on the Mount: "Anyone who nurses anger against his brother must be brought to judgement" (Matt. 5:22).

The point is this: Whether it be our brothers or our spouses, resentment is not where we *begin;* it is where we *arrive.* After making a considerable journey, it is a condition that gradually develops over time. It is anger with a history. If we get to this destination at all, it is by violating the admonitions of Scripture.

No Surprises with Resentment

Spouses enter affairs from a variety of marriages. These marriages may seem very different, but one thing they share in common is a failing nature. If these failing relationships were placed on a continuum according to the couples' level of awareness of their failing condition, we would find marriages scattered from one extreme to the other. For instance, some marriages fail very subtly. Possibly the deterioration has been so gradual that failure was even beyond the awareness of both partners. They just gradually and methodically drifted apart. After all, the normal preoccupations of life kept them busy—making a living, raising a family, keeping a household running. The ordinary demands of everyday life can have an extraordinary effect on marriages. Realization of their relational failure may have come only with the unpremeditated crisis of betrayal.

Other marriages fail with greater fanfare—there is nothing subtle about it. These marriages are characterized by arguing, bickering, and other acts of combativeness; abuse in one form or another; or overt relational neglect and behavioral irresponsibility. There are clearly demonstrated, repetitive acts of insensitivity. The overt disrespect and hostility which played itself out over the years leaves no surprises regarding the presence of marital dissatisfaction.

Somewhere between these two extremes—the subtle and the obvious—the remaining cases of marital betrayal are found. Marriages in which offender-resentment is a problem are always found toward the more obvious end of this continuum. There are no surprises. Possibly the failing nature was not apparent to both of the partners. A dissatisfied spouse may have sullenly kept the secret to himself. But at least one of the spouses has been dissatisfied, and this discontent has been both known and brewing for a considerable length of time. This unresolved dissatisfaction, whether the wounds were intentional or not, finally consummates in an attitude of resentment. And this resentment is the block to restoration.

Mary and Steve

It was one of those summers where I had the opportunity to take more than one family vacation. I spent two weeks in the mountains of Colorado and, after a month back in the office, took two more weeks off to relax at the beach. You may be wondering what my summer vacation schedule has to do with marital betrayal. Nothing directly, but indirectly, an interesting pattern emerged with one of the couples with whom I had been counseling. Each time I went on vacation with my family, Steve had taken a vacation from his marriage.

Steve and Mary had come to me by way of professional referral. Steve had been involved in an affair with a woman at work for nearly a year before Mary discovered the relationship. She was totally surprised. Not only was this so out of character for Steve—a highly respected member of the community and responsible family man—but Mary had also not detected even the slightest hint of marital dissatisfaction. She knew Steve was unhappy with work and sensed he was struggling with questions of where exactly his life was headed. But the marriage? Mary had had no idea that Steve was displeased, much less involved in betrayal.

Following the discovery of infidelity and a brief separation, the decision was made to end the affair and preserve the marriage. It was this decision that brought Mary and Steve to me. We had worked through the early stages of the counseling process. We understood the marital history that had led to relational deterioration; we knew the natural interferences. We had tensely discussed the affair—all the pain and hurt. We had made full disclosure, making certain that there were no unanswered questions lurking about to sabotage the progress of restoration. We had embraced reconciliation with Steve reporting a degree of remorse. We had even dealt with a block to restoration prompted by Mary's resentment of the betrayal. She finally had faced and resolved her bitterness.

It seemed, having successfully resolved the affair, that we were ready to face the marriage. Yet progress, if any, was slow. The interruption in a weekly counseling process necessitated by my vacations only served to illuminate what may have otherwise remained hidden. When Mary and Steve were seen on a regular basis, there appeared to be some progress. At least they were dealing with each other in session. However, without our weekly meetings, the lack of effort on Steve's part became glaring.

This was our first session after my second vacation. It had been several weeks since we had last met. I began with a customary question: "How are things going with Mary and Steve?" Mary was quick to share both her concern and displeasure. She was obviously frustrated with Steve's lack of investment in the marriage.

Steve's been on vacation too. Every time you leave town, so does he. At least he leaves as far as the marriage is concerned.

I don't know what to do. He just withdraws. He's cordial if we have to speak, but that's it. We're not talking about anything important. He's not sharing his feelings with me, and he's definitely not dealing with any dissatisfactions. I have no idea what's going on in his head. It's just like it was during the affair.

Steve didn't respond. He just sat quietly in his chair. I sensed Mary was correct. They were stuck. But why? What's stopping this couple from working on their marriage? Is it the discomfort that comes from facing the natural interferences themselves? Or is it resistance? Is it actually a blockage from the affair—something that had not yet been resolved? Whether a discomfort or a blockage, the problem seemed to rest with Steve. It was Steve who was not cooperating; it was Steve who held the answers to my questions.

What's the problem, Steve? What's stopping you from dealing with your marriage? Why the hesitancy?

After a long pause, Steve finally responded, "I don't know." I believe that "I don't know" usually means "I don't want to say." Knowing Steve's personality and behavioral tendencies, I felt fairly certain he had the answers to my questions. He just preferred to avoid in session what he had successfully avoided at home. I decided to press for an answer.

Usually when people say they don't know something, they actually do. I suspect that's the case with you, Steve. Now, really, what's going on? What's stopping you from dealing with Mary and your marriage?

My question was followed by another long pause. Steve sat motionless, but I could tell his mind was feverishly working. Time continued to pass. I was determined to outwait him. Finally, Steve broke the silence.

The focus of what we've done in counseling has been on the affair. That was wrong of me. I know that. I did a bad thing—and I really mean that. But there has been far more to our marriage than just the last year, and there has been far more than the affair.

I don't think I've really been heard in our marriage for a long time. She heard my words, but that was it. What I had to say, what I wanted, didn't really matter. I might as well have been talking to the wall.

Do you know how it feels to not count in your own home—to not have any real say? Well, it made me mad, and I'm still mad about it.

Mary was hurt by what I did. For that I'm sorry. But I was hurt too! Not just during this last year but over the past several years. I don't hear anyone talking about that.

Here was our blockage. Steve said he was mad. However, long ago he had passed being simply mad and moved into being bitter. Whereas Mary had been wounded by the incident of betrayal, Steve had a "pattern wound." It had not been a single incident that hurt him but his perception of being repetitively discounted. Each reenactment only served to etch more deeply the resentment he was nursing. When we finally got past the "I don't know's" to emotional honesty, what came forth from this otherwise self-controlled husband was a venomous line of verbal attacks. It was like opening a box. Everything that had been tightly kept inside was spilling out.

Mary was stunned. Her mind was in a whirl. Not only was she unused to this kind of emotional intensity from Steve, but Mary was also confused. She did not understand the source of Steve's accusations. Steve began to elaborate. He spoke of how Mary never took seriously his concerns for their financial future. He felt his desire for her to seek full-time employment was dismissed. His views regarding the children seemed to carry little weight. And his complaint of being deprioritized when their children were born did not result in any change in Mary's behavior. At least this was how Steve viewed their marital history, and it was upon this perception that his bitterness was based. He also had been hurt!

These were not new topics. They first emerged early in the counseling process as we tried to explore Mary and Steve's history and exactly how the marriage was allowed to get to a point of failure. We had discussed Steve's dissatisfactions. What we had discovered was that things were not as simple as he presented. His feelings were true enough, but his perception of Mary as being blatantly insensitive did not seem to be accurate.

Steve had enjoyed the early years of marriage—the childless years. Things were easier then. He liked the attention that came with being the only other person in the relationship. Financial stresses were less. But children transform couples into families, and this always requires adaptation on the part of spouses. Mary had had an easier time making the necessary changes than Steve. This, coupled with Steve's tendency to avoid conflict, laid the groundwork for his complaints. Mary remembered occasional discussions of these issues, but she remembered them as being discussed and resolved. She was totally unaware of Steve's apparent early withdrawal from the conflict, and she definitely had been unaware of his continued dissatisfactions. In Mary's mind, Steve had been heard. In Steve's, he had not. And it was his perception that created his resentment.

So these were not new topics, but apparently they continued to be unresolved. Steve had not demonstrated his resentment overtly; he had not confronted Mary. He just passively resisted. Unless pushed, he did nothing. But doing nothing effectively blocked their progress.

Intervention

As with any form of resentment, Steve would either face his bitterness and let it go, or it would consume him and continue to control his life. He would need to clearly identify what he believed to be the wound and who caused the wound. He would need to recognize and admit to the pain this had caused him. He would need to express all of this to the one who had hurt him instead of sullenly holding it within. Then he would need to choose to let it go—to choose forgiveness over hostility.

Having faced both the pain and the culprit, Steve would be freed to face the future. I knew this cognitively, and to some extent, so did Steve. However, as I have already stated, the art of therapy is not necessarily knowing what people ought to do, it is in getting them to do it. What Steve needed to do was clear. Whether I could help him to deal with Mary and then let his bitterness go was the question. I chose to be confrontive and prescribed a task for Steve and Mary to complete at home.

Steve, I want you to go home and be heard. You know what needs to be said—what's stuffed down inside of you crying to get out. Go home and let it out. Mary wants to hear what you think, how you've been hurt, and how you feel. She wants to know, so go tell her.

Take about an hour in the privacy of your home. Set a timer for fifteen-minute intervals. During that time, you can say what you've been wanting to say for years. Mary will not interrupt you. After the fifteen minutes, she will have three minutes to respond. She will not defend or attack but will only report back to you what she is hearing you say. She needs to hear you. Do this three times during your hour. Then report back to me. We'll deal in here with cleaning up what was said.

Get out of character, Steve. Deal honestly with Mary. Get some volume–yell a little bit. Work up some anger. Pound some pillows. Do what it takes to let her know how you feel.

Steve was a little shocked with my prescription. He was also resistant. His hesitancy was clothed in overprotective terms like, "I'm afraid I may say some things that will hurt Mary beyond repair." I suspected a truer motivation was self-protection. Steve feared Mary's response.

Steve, there is nothing you can say that will hurt Mary any worse than what you are doing now. She can heal from your remarks, but she cannot heal from what you do not say.

Deal with your resentment. Face it and let it go. Then, Steve, grow up and move on with your life!

To this point, my prescription had been direct and instructional, but it had not necessarily been confrontive. The tone of my intervention suddenly changed. Suggesting that Steve needed to grow up was an aggressive remark. It hurt his feelings. This was my intent though not my goal. I am reminded of a statement made by Paul in his second letter to the church at Corinth. He had apparently said some things in his first letter that had been offensive.

> Even if I did wound you by the letter I sent, I do not now regret it. I may have been sorry for it when I saw that the letter had caused you pain, even if only for a time; but now I am happy, not that your feelings were wounded but that the wound led to a change of heart.
>
> 2 Corinthians 7:8–9

I do not enjoy inflicting pain or, to use Paul's terminology, wounding people. But sometimes it takes the stress encountered by being wounded to give impetus for following through on what needs to be done. That was my rationale with this intervention. Steve already knew what he needed to do. My prescription only gave him an identifiable structure. It gave him permission to vent. However, I questioned whether he would really complete the task. So I wounded him. Pointing out the immaturity of someone who fails to live responsibly was my extra nudge. In this instance, it proved effective.

Relationships are complex. For relationships to grow, resentment and bitterness must be resolved. Regardless of who is holding onto the hurt, failing to let go of resentment only maintains a couple in a state of suspension. It may be that some couples will only need to be made aware of the blockage, then they will choose to face, deal, resolve, and move on. Others may require a little more artful assistance. Regardless, bitterness is a block to marital restoration and one way or another has to be dismissed for restoration to occur.

Quick-Scan 10

Things to remember about offender resentment

✓ Determine that the impasse rests with the offender's unwillingness to release past hurts—to extend forgiveness for historical aspects of the marital relationship. (Differentiate from the attitude of justification, which fails to accept personal wrongdoing.)

✓ Resentment is an unhealthy mutation of a natural emotion. It is anger with a history.

✓ Resentment comes as no surprise to the offender. His dissatisfactions have been present for a considerable period of time.

✓ The resentment must be faced and resolved.

- Help the offender identify the wound(s).
- Help the offender identify who caused the wound.
- Help the offender identify the extent of his pain.
- Help the offender express all of these.
- Encourage the offender to *choose* to let it go.

✓ Apply pressure if necessary.

14

"I Can't Let Her Go!"

I had met with Paige sporadically over a period of six months. Counseling was precipitated by her husband's decision to leave the marriage and immediately file for divorce. Reid claimed he had gradually grown tired of their relationship. After months of deliberation, he had finally come to the conclusion that there was nothing left for him to do but to move on with his life. As he had expressed it to Paige: "I'm really doing us a favor. In the long run, this will be best for us both. You deserve someone who really loves you."

Paige was initially surprised by what appeared to be such an abrupt decision on Reid's part. She was not surprised with Reid's dissatisfaction. She knew he had not been totally satisfied with the marriage for quite some time. For that matter, she had not been satisfied either. But to suddenly be so dissatisfied as to want an immediate termination? Paige suspected that more than mere discontent with her was at the core of Reid's request. It was her suspicion that Reid was involved with another woman.

Paige did not dispute Reid's dissatisfaction, only his true motivation. Rather than being a pushed-out husband, a spouse whose motivation to leave is based upon feeling emotionally frustrated and trapped, she viewed Reid as being pulled out, a spouse whose motivation to leave is based upon an emotional attachment or pull toward someone outside of the marriage.

(These and other aspects of marital crisis are thoroughly presented in my book *When the One You Love Wants to Leave* [Baker Book House, 1993.]) When Paige confronted Reid with her suspicions, he was quick to deny any such involvement. He continued to assert, "I'm just tired of our marriage."

As a clinician, I had suspicions similar to those of Paige. Not knowing all of the facts, my concurrence with her assessment of Reid's motivation to leave was admittedly speculative. However, I have found that there are some characteristics which tend to help differentiate between spouses being either pushed or pulled out of a marriage. One of the most significant differences is the departing spouse's haste to pursue the legal dissolution of the marriage. People who are pushed out of a marriage are not usually anxious to pursue divorce. Confusion seems to be one of their prime characteristics. They are uncertain about most everything in their lives, of what they want to see happen with the marriage, with their spouse, and with themselves. The only thing of which there seems to be any certainty at all is their desire for space. They want some alone time—an opportunity to think things through and figure out what it is that they do want.

This can be sharply contrasted with those who leave a marriage for another person. To make as drastic and paramount a decision as that leaves little room in their mind regarding confusion. These spouses know what they want—the other person. In their minds, it is the other person who makes them feel good and who will bring them happiness. They are anxious to pursue this new relationship to an even greater degree. Thus, there is the need for an expedient resolution to their current marriage.

Not every spouse who is being pulled out of a marriage admits to this fact. It is still more socially acceptable to be pushed than pulled—to want to leave a marriage because of dissatisfaction, incompatibility, the failure to meet each other's needs, etc., than to leave for another person. So rather than admit to infidelity, some spouses prefer to follow one deception with another. They first deceive their spouse through betrayal. This deception is then followed by claiming their motivation for leaving is, "I'm just tired of our marriage."

Reid's departure had all the markings of betrayal as opposed to frustration. He was too quick to know what he wanted. Also, this was not the first instance of betrayal in their marriage. As if Reid was following a script, the scenario that was being played out was identical to that of an earlier experience. The classic signs were there—haste to pursue divorce, secrecy regarding where he was living, large periods of time when his whereabouts were unaccounted for—but more importantly for Paige, these were all things that she had seen before. Five years earlier, Reid had stated his dissatisfaction with the marriage, that he just did not love Paige. Then, too, he denied any other involvement, but time proved his denial to be false. There had been another woman then, and Paige was certain there was another woman this time as well.

During the course of nearly six months, Reid and Paige's marriage had moved precariously close to a divorce. However, with legal actions set in motion, Reid suddenly changed his mind and requested the opportunity to pursue reconciliation. Paige was surprised and in many ways found herself to be hesitant. She questioned whether she was actually setting herself up to be hurt once again. After all, what had really been going on with Reid since their separation, and what were his true motivations for wanting to return? It was during a time of relational soul-searching that Reid admitted to having had an affair. Paige's suspicions had been accurate, but he assured her that this illicit relationship was over. Reid said he was back to stay and that he desperately wanted to work on rebuilding their marriage. With some reluctance, Paige decided to give Reid and the marriage one last chance.

Over the next several weeks, Reid did little to relieve any of Paige's fears. Though Reid's whereabouts were never in question, he didn't seem to be any more interested in spending time with Paige than he had prior to their separation. He was still more invested in activities that kept him away from the home. Even when he was at home, his interests seemed to exclude

Paige. But what really bothered her was Reid's attitude and some of the requests he was making.

I was already questioning Reid's real desire to be back home because of some of his behavior. Nothing had changed. He was still gone all the time. He even seemed to look for excuses to be out of the house. That didn't seem to me to be the behavior of someone who was wanting the marriage to be different than it had been. But what really let me know that things weren't totally over between Reid and Terri were some of the things he was asking me to do.

Reid wanted me to call Terri and assure her that I had forgiven her for what she had done. He almost became insistent about this. When I seemed hesitant, he would start talking about how sorry he felt for her—that she was having such a hard time getting over the breakup. There was also the matter of some unreturned property. When Reid moved out, he had taken a stereo, a television, and a VCR with him. These are still at Terri's place. Sure, I am concerned about the expense involved in replacing these items. They serve a functional role in our home. But I am more concerned with the principle. These are our things, not hers, but Reid refuses to get them back. He keeps saying that Terri needs them, and he doesn't want to hurt her any more than she has already been hurt.

Reid's not really back! He's home, but I don't know why. He may not be seeing Terri, but it is obvious that he still cares for her. In fact, he seems to care far more about her feelings than he does mine. This just isn't right!

Paige was frustrated with Reid's behavior. She was also hurt by what she deemed to be his double-minded attitude—continuing to care for Terri while supposedly recommitted to his marriage. In both cases, Paige's concerns were legitimate. As she had assessed, Reid was not really back. He was home physically, but his heart was at least confused, if not truly still with Terri. I refer to this as a *lingering attachment.*

Reid was not actually maintaining the adulterous relationship with Terri. As he had promised, the affair had ended. Yet even though the minimum prerequisites for restoration were met, Reid's continued emotional pull toward Terri brought restoration for the marriage to a grinding halt. Without a change in Reid's double-mindedness—without some resolution of his lingering attachment to Terri—his relationship with Paige would remain stuck.

Lingering Attachment

A lingering attachment is the continuation of an emotional bond between the partners of an affair after the illicit relationship has ended. Sometimes the lingering attachment is mutual. Neither of the individuals resolved their feelings for each other prior to the termination of the affair. This is frequently the case when one or both decides that ending the relationship is the most responsible, moral, or financially beneficial course of action. At other times, the continued attachment is one-sided. This is the case when one partner resolves his or her feelings and decides to end the relationship regardless of how the other individual may feel. The rejected partner, who still has unresolved feelings for the former lover, may then choose to return to his or her spouse.

Not every incidence of betrayal will result in a lingering attachment. But for those returning spouses for whom resolution has yet to occur, complications in restoration can be expected. Feelings can be tenacious, and they are not respectful of the *shoulds, oughts,* and preferences of our lives. The fact that a spouse shouldn't feel romantically toward an individual outside of the marriage, or that he ought to feel deeply and affectionately toward his wife, or that he wishes that his emotions were different does not always change how he really feels. And how he really feels is the problem. To get past the blockage for restoration, the lingering attachment—how he really feels—must be resolved.

If we lived in an ideal world, there would be no affairs. Even if there were, they would all end cleanly, with no lingering attachments. However, life is seldom ideal. It is unrealistic to anticipate that all spouses who return to a marriage do so completely ready to work on restoration—completely over the other man or woman. As counselors, we are called upon to face reality. This is not a time to give up, but a time to intervene.

Intervention

In treating what may appear to be a lingering attachment, it is important to determine that what remains between the offender and the former lover is just the emotional bond. If the illicit relationship is still active, though deceptively hidden, there is more at stake than lingering emotions. Making this determination is not always an easy task. In the absence of proof to the contrary, it is generally best to proceed as if the affair truly is terminated, trusting that if this is not the case, the truth will eventually be demonstrated. (If progress continues to be impeded, it may be worth further investigation. A deceptively maintained affair will prevent movement in restoration.)

Once it is determined that the problem is truly one of lingering emotional attachment, intervention can proceed. When presented with this problem, spouses can be placed in one of two categories. They either have significant *personal issues* operating deep within, or they have yet to *completely grieve the loss* of the illicit relationship. Your role as a counselor will vary depending upon which of these two situations actually exists.

Personal Issues

I had counseled with Elizabeth and Paul for several months. We had supposedly worked through the crisis precipitated by the affair and were dealing with some of the historical relationship issues. From all appearances, progress was being made. Both were investing more time and energy into the marriage.

Paul voiced no complaints, and Elizabeth was delighted with the increased amount of time together. Then Elizabeth arrived for our weekly appointment without Paul.

He's gone back to Lois—again. I came home from work to find his clothes gone and a note:

Elizabeth,
    I know this will hurt you, but I can't get Lois out of my mind. It's like I am addicted to her.
    I don't know what I'm going to do. But for now, I'm moving back with her. Please forgive me. I'll call you later.
                                                                    Paul

I don't know what to do. How can I fight an addiction? Even if Paul does decide to return and to give us another chance, how can I ever trust him again? I just don't know what to do.

Elizabeth was discouraged. Things had been going so well. A relapse of this nature caught her completely by surprise. What was Paul thinking? Why did he leave her again? As we attempted to make some sense out of what had just taken place, the picture that began to emerge of Paul was one that was far less flattering than had previously been suggested.

Initially, Paul's affair was viewed as unpremeditated and a by-product of his dissatisfaction with his marriage. By nature, Paul was conflict avoidant. Rather than dealing directly with Elizabeth regarding the aspects of their marriage which he found to be troublesome, he pretended everything was fine. He had hoped his complaints would magically disappear. The consequence of avoidance is predictable. In counseling, we had identified the old patterns and were making efforts to bring change. The rationale was, if dissatisfactions could be directly resolved, there would be less potential for marital discord.

Though this plan of action sounded appropriate, it assumed that Paul was emotionally healthier than he actually was. There was more to Paul, and to his difficulties, than mere tendencies toward conflict avoidance. There were some deep longings for love and acceptance, longings which surpassed normal and legitimate needs and expectations, which Paul believed could only be met by the other woman. Though his intellectual system would bring him back home to Elizabeth and his marriage, the depth of his emotional neediness would pull him back toward Lois, the woman Paul felt could fill the emptiness in his life.

The cause of this form of emptiness is variable. When encountered, it is imperative that both the excessiveness of the need and the severity of the problem be recognized. This is actually more than a mere lingering attachment. The problem is much deeper. These forms of personal issues will require intensive individual therapy to be resolved. Unless this is an area in which you are highly skilled, referral to an appropriate professional is the best option. True restoration will not likely continue until the in-depth issues are resolved.

Uncompleted Grief

Unlike those offenders with significant personal issues, the problem of uncompleted grief can be associated with a more normal or ordinary population. Grief, an individual's response to loss, is a natural response. And grieving, the process whereby the emotions surrounding the loss are resolved, is also natural. It makes little difference whether the relationship which has been lost was illicit or legitimate—it still represents loss. A successful resolution of the loss is required for an offender to let the relationship go.

As a counselor, aiding an offender in resolving the lingering attachment frequently requires that you assist him or her to grieve the loss. This would best be accomplished in individual sessions. Sometimes helping in the grief process requires you to be a listener. At other times, more directive action is called for. It is important to realize that grieving is a process. As such, though there can be gradual improvement, instantaneous change is unlikely. In aiding an offender to emotionally release the illicit relationship, it is beneficial to recognize some of the factors which aid or help the resolution of grief.

The passage of time. There is an old adage that states, "Time heals all wounds." Like most old adages, there are both elements of truth and untruth found in this statement. Time, in and of itself, will not necessarily heal all wounds. Some of the things that bring pain to our lives continue to do so in spite of the passage of months or even years. This is not necessarily healthy, nor is it inevitable, but it can be reality. Similar to physical wounds, unattended emotional hurts can also fail to properly heal if not adequately cleansed. If the particular wound were to be an instance of loss, this failure to heal over time would represent what is referred to as *pathological grief.*

Pathological grief does not heal with time. However, in instances of loss where everything that is supposed to be done is actually accomplished, there is some healing which will come through no other means than the passage of time. This emphasizes the process nature of grieving—there is not instantaneous relief. Release of the former relationship can, and usually does, come, but it will take a while.

The normality of this process can often be a difficult thing for the rejected and offended spouse to accept. After all, what the offender is having difficulty resolving was illicit. "He shouldn't feel that way." However, the illicit nature of the relationship does not change the fact that something of an emotional nature existed between the offender and the other man or woman. Though illicit, it still represents loss; loss necessitates grieving; and grieving requires the passage of time.

Embracing reality. Sometimes what holds an offender to an affair is an overidealized perspective of the former lover. He remembers all of the good times that they had together and recalls only the most positive qualities of the other person. Fantasized dreams of a life together continue to inundate his imagination.

I am not saying that there were not some enjoyable times or that the other person really had no redeeming qualities. To take that position would be as blatant a form of denial as is represented by the overidealization. What is needed is for the offender to embrace reality. He needs to accept the fact that there were bad times as well as good, that the former lover had negative qualities as well as positive, and that their dreams together were just that—dreams, and most dreams are fictional.

There are no knights in shining armor—there are no maidens to rescue. Everyone has chinks in their armor, and every relationship has blemishes. Affairs are no different. What may have been different for the affair was the lack of real-life pressure. This may have protected them to some degree. Add to this the extraordinary excitement that often accompanies acts of deception, and you find betrayal to exist in an artificial hothouse environment. Still, a realistic assessment of the situation typically brings a more moderate stance.

In attempting to bring an offender face-to-face with reality, I prefer to utilize writing exercises. The offender is given the assignment to begin compiling a list of the good *and* the bad times together, the positive *and* the negative attributes of the former lover, and what would have been the *realistic* anticipations and consequences of a life together. I caution the offender: "If all you can find are positive things to say, then you're continuing to live in a fantasy world." As he or she begins to earnestly develop the list, and as we then discuss and process the findings in session, there is a gradual move away from the overidealization. The offender begins to embrace reality.

Obtaining closure. Some emotional attachments linger because there has never been an actual act of closure. Instead of the relationship having a formal ending, the termination was either abrupt and one-sided or left hanging in a state of suspended animation. With the *abruptly ended* form of (non)closure, the offender feels rejected. For whatever reason, his former lover decided to end the affair and dump him. Sometimes this is handled with a telephone call or a letter. Occasionally, it is even accomplished in a brief face-to-face meeting. What is characteristic of this form of closure is the unexpected nature in which the termination arose and the swiftness in which it was executed. In a very confused state, the rejected lover retains a sense of there having been many things left unsaid.

To aid in resolving this tie to the past, I encourage the offender to make an opportunity to bring closure to the affair—to ask any questions that he may still have and to express whatever it is that he believes needs to be stated. Ideally, the former lover will cooperate in some type of formal exercise. This can be in a neutral and public setting and without the participation of any significant others. (Having spouses present would interfere with what needs to occur. The goal is not to reconcile the illicit relationship but to bring closure to it. This is best accomplished with no other onlookers.) In lieu of any cooperation or participation on the part of the former lover, letter writing is the next best alternative. Though the answers to questions may not be as readily received from a letter, at least they can be asked, and writing will also offer opportunity for expression.

It is important that either the meeting or the letter be a once-and-for-all exercise. This must be clearly stated at the outset. The goal is closure, not continuation. The spouse must be certain to deal with everything at one time. After the meeting, there should be nothing remaining for resolution—no new questions, no new hostile remarks, no further good-byes. Nothing is to be left unsaid.

Unlike the relationship which ended abruptly, a relationship which encounters a *nebulous ending* probably did include a face-to-face discussion. This effort toward dissolving the affair, however, lacked clarity. Tim's experience illustrates the problem inherent in a nebulous ending.

Calling off the affair was the best thing to do. We both knew it was the right choice. But when we decided to go back and deal with our marriages, neither of us knew exactly what to expect. What if things didn't work out at home? What if Shannon couldn't accept me back? What if we just couldn't make it work? Trish and I had really felt something for each other. It was hard to completely burn our bridges. As much as we still cared for each other, I was hesitant to say anything that might really hurt her feelings. So we left things kind of open-ended.

I haven't seen Trish in over a month. But as loosely as things were left between us, I still feel connected to her. I don't know that we completely settled anything when we decided to call the affair quits.

Tim and Trish had never reached closure on their illicit relationship. They kind of, sort of, almost ended the affair, but not really. Theirs was not the problem of the abruptly ended relationship—there were no questions to be asked or angry sentiments to be expressed. But there needed to be a clear statement of good-bye.

Similar to the abruptly ended variation of a failed closure, this can be accomplished either in person, over the telephone, or through the mail. What is important is that there be clarification—a statement that leaves no question as to the status of the former relationship. It is definitely and absolutely terminated. Neither Tim nor Trish needs to continue with any false hope that the affair looms in the background as a relational safety net. Clearly, it has ended.

Making a firm resolve. Sandra had ended her relationship with James several weeks earlier. At least she thought she had. "I had hoped it would run its course, making it easy for me. But it hasn't. I still feel attached." Time alone had not taken care of Sandra's feelings for James. Though not much time had yet passed, Sandra was concerned that whatever it was that she had felt for James did not seem to be lessening. "How do you make yourself do what you don't feel like doing?"

That was a good question. What might be a better question is, "By what will your life be controlled—emotions or reason?" Professionals generally agree that emotions are strong and definitely need to be recognized, evaluated, and weighed when it comes to making decisions. However, emotions alone should never be allowed to control one's behavior. An emotionally oriented individual is bound for heartache and mishap. Decisions and behavior need to be based on sound, rational judgment.

It is always easier to do something that you feel like doing. It is always difficult to do what you do not feel like doing, but feelings alone should never be the final indicator for making any decisions. Sometimes you are left to make a choice based on fact, and you have to trust that if you make the right choice and then do everything else that is healthy and correct to do, that time will eventually work in your best interest to bring about the corresponding emotional response.

That proved to be the case with Sandra. She resolved in her heart to let the relationship with James go. She did not deny her feelings for him, but she recognized the faultiness in them. Upon arriving at a firm resolve, beginning to embrace reality, and executing a final act of closure, the passage of time began to effectively deal with Sandra's lingering emotions. Gradually, but noticeably, the attachment was broken and Sandra was freed to pursue restoration.

A lingering attachment is frustrating. It is seldom desired, often resisted, and occasionally deviant, but it is also resolvable. Successfully dealing with this block to restoration may necessitate some significant personal work—delving into the deep and core issues which seem to tie an individual to a past love. In a healthier vein, it may require one or more of the helps to completing the grieving of the loss—finalizing the act of letting go. Regardless of the category, as a counselor, you have a role to play. This, too, is an opportunity for you to be a part of the restoration process.

Quick-Scan 11

Things to remember about a lingering attachment

✓ A lingering attachment is the continuation of an emotional bond between the partners of an affair after the illicit relationship has ended.

✓ Be certain that it is only the emotional bond, and not the actual relationship, that continues to linger.

✓ Determine the category of the bond.

- Are there significant *personal issues* operating deep within the spouse?
- Has he or she failed to *completely grieve the loss* of the illicit relationship?

✓ The presence of significant personal issues will necessitate in-depth therapy.

✓ The presence of an uncompleted grief process will necessitate assistance in facing the loss. This will involve all or part of the following:

- The passage of time
- Embracing reality
- Obtaining closure
- Making a firm resolve

Part **4**

Restoring the Marriage

15

What *Was* Still *Is*

I had met with Jerry and Rita for several sessions over a period of two months. The early sessions were characterized by emotional intensity. Rita was by nature an expressive woman. She was animated and easily excited. Jerry was far more easygoing—a man who could aptly be described as gentle. He was not a weak individual, but his gentle nature, marked by a tendency to be too nice, often found him overprotecting those around him. He worked hard at not hurting the feelings of others.

At the beginning of our counseling, both Jerry and Rita questioned whether their marriage could be saved. Jerry had betrayed Rita's trust by having an affair several years earlier. Discovery of the infidelity had prompted a separation. After six months of living apart, Jerry decided to end the adulterous relationship, and he and Rita agreed to resume the marriage. On their own, they agreed to let the affair be a part of the past and to begin a new phase of their marriage. Unfortunately, the optimism which fueled their new beginning was not of sufficient power to keep Rita's unresolved feelings of hurt and betrayal from interfering with their marriage. Periodically Rita's suppressed emotions would go unchecked, resulting in an intense verbal altercation. This would be followed by a period of silence and avoidance as each gathered their emotional wits. After several days of not speaking, the silence would be broken. Jerry and Rita would then resume cordial behavior, each pretending nothing had occurred. The cordiality phase would continue until something triggered another reaction in Rita, once again moving the relationship to overt hostility.

For two years, this cycle had repeated itself. Neither wanted it—neither could control it. I was struck by their weary appearance and fatigue. The last two years had been hard on both Jerry and Rita. Much like a shoreline shows the wear of the ocean's constant pounding, so did this relationship. The repetitive nature of the cycle was gradually causing a deterioration in how Jerry and Rita felt toward each other. They were becoming disillusioned—losing hope that things could ever be any different. Was change beyond what they could accomplish on their own? Was it even possible with outside intervention? These were the questions they brought to counseling, and each honestly shared doubts regarding any long-term future for the marriage.

In examining the marital history, a clear scenario emerged. What they had brought into the marriage as natural tendencies quickly formed some interactional patterns which worked against the healthy development of an intimate relationship. Rita was goal directed. Sometimes her persistence in accomplishing a task clouded her vision for what was needed in her marriage. This was not intentional, but it impacted the marriage nonetheless. Jerry was too nice. He did not like conflict and liked hurting the feelings of others even less. So rather than dealing with his feelings of dissatisfaction in the marriage, he smiled and went on as if everything was fine. Rita's tendency to be emotionally reactive and Jerry's discomfort with intense emotions only helped him with his decision to be avoidant.

What appeared to be a workable solution for Jerry and Rita slowly proved to be ineffective. With time, Jerry's dissatisfaction began to harden. His anger turned to resentment. Though walls began to grow in the marriage, Rita was too busy to notice, and Jerry was too nice to point them out. At least no one noticed until the betrayal.

As Jerry and Rita shared their marital history, the cooperative pattern of insensitivity and avoidance brought understanding. It did not bring justification, but it did explain how what began in commitment and love could degenerate to the sordidness of infidelity.

I knew what needed to happen for Jerry and Rita to move toward restoration. They needed to face and resolve the affair that had brought crisis to their marriage. There needed to be ownership; there needed to be disclosure; and there needed to be forgiveness. What followed were some tense times as we methodically worked through the circumstances surrounding the betrayal. Strong feelings were shared by both Jerry and Rita. But with the achievement of a genuine reconciliation, a corner was turned in their marriage. They were able to place the betrayal in the past and to move toward the future.

As the betrayal was resolved and Jerry and Rita began to look toward the reconstruction of their marriage, something began to break in upon their awareness. Rita began to realize that she was still goal directed, intense, and somewhat insensitive toward Jerry's needs. As for Jerry, he saw where he was still conflict avoidant. "We've noticed that the same patterns that were in our marriage before the affair are still there. We're surprised. Is that normal?"

Earlier in the counseling process, I had informed Jerry and Rita in a general manner that we would have to resolve the affair before we could deal with the marriage, but that dealing with the marriage was our ultimate goal. Sometimes you tell people something but they don't really comprehend it until they experience it. That seemed to be true for this couple. We had resolved the affair. With it truly in the past, they were ready to look at the marriage. As they did, the flaws became obvious. What was even more obvious was the reality of my principle regarding marital crisis: What *was* still *is*.

For Jerry and Rita, *it was marital crisis that brought them to counseling, but it was their tendencies toward insensitivity and avoidance that brought them to crisis.* We had successfully resolved the crisis. Now it was time to face the marriage. If we did not successfully resolve the issues that had cooperatively led to the crisis, there was no reason to believe that the problems of the marriage would not be replicated at a later date. What was still is, and the tendencies needed to be resolved.

Effecting a Transition

To continue the work of restoring the marriage, a transition must be made from the affair to the relationship. Earlier pitfalls for counseling involved either too little or too much focus on the affair. Tendencies were to either avoid the affair or to obsess about it. With the affair being resolved, the therapeutic situation changes. The pitfall which now confronts you is whether the couple will continue the counseling process at all. With resolution of betrayal, there is a real tendency for a couple to drop out of counseling. After all, reconciliation has brought an improved relationship. They are not only treating each other better, but there is also a change in the emotional tone of the marriage. A couple typically thinks: "Things are better. Why not bask in the accomplishments that have been achieved and just allow the marriage to proceed?"

Though the bulk of this book has focused on the essential task of resolving the affair, the bulk of your counseling efforts will be spent after this has occurred. Reconciliation has to come first. Ideally, this resolution will be accomplished in a minimal amount of time. However, if you are to be truly successful in restoring this marriage, it will be the work that follows the reconciliation that will bring this to pass. The couple must deal with their relationship. At this crucial step in the restoration process, you may have to sell the couple on their need for further counseling.

Effecting a transition in focus is aided by stressing the "what was still is" philosophy. You do this both generally and specifically. The problem must become very real to the couple. This is accomplished by identifying the characteristics that have operated in their marriage prior to the affair. What were the factors that interfered with growth? Clearly articulate what each spouse did or did not do. The better you can describe the scenario for their marital failure and support the reality of the present-tense occurrence of these same tendencies, the greater the opportunity for continuing the counseling process.

Dealing with the Relationship

It could take an entire book to discuss how to deal with the interferences in the marriage—the actual individual characteristics and interactional patterns that have inhibited growth in the past and, if unchecked, will prevent the marriage from moving toward a healthy and emotionally bonded union in the future. The focus of this book has been to get you successfully to this point. Now there is opportunity to conduct what would be considered more traditional marital therapy. Insensitivity, avoidance tendencies, inappropriate or conflicting expectations, inequities in power structures—these are just some of the issues that create problems for couples and are likely to be found in the marriages brought to a point of crisis by betrayal.

Resolving the affair is a new beginning; it is not a place to stop. This is an opportunity for a couple to truly enrich their marriage. As you begin to focus on the relationship, there are two lingering aspects of the betrayal which may rise up to dampen your efforts. For the betrayed spouse, trust commonly continues to be an issue. For the offender, impatience with the amount of time involved in the natural process of healing may prove to be disruptive. In addition to problems for the spouses, counselors are also tempted with some natural pitfalls. These lingering problems for couples and counselors will be the final focus of this book. Though they may require some attention, do not let them distract you from your new goal. Now is the time to truly practice the art of therapy and to direct a couple to the new task at hand—enriching and restoring their marriage.

16

"How Can I Ever Trust Again?"

It would be the unusual couple who would not have some lingering difficulties with trust within their marriage. A problem of trust within a marriage obviously affects the relationship as a whole, but it is the betrayed spouse who experiences the greater difficulty with trust. It is the offended spouse who must risk being vulnerable again. The memories of the pain of betrayal, much less the incident itself, cannot be erased. If trust returns to a marriage, it does so in spite of the past and not because it has been totally eliminated.

Trust issues are common. Even in marriages where both spouses are doing everything within their power to bring restoration to the relationship, trust can continue to be an issue for a considerable length of time. For the issue of trust to be successfully resolved, several things must occur. First, there must be an appropriate atmosphere established. This involves prerequisites that foster an *environment for growth.* Second, there must be actions on the part of the offending spouse demonstrating reasons for the continuation of trust. Though an offender can never do enough to earn trust, there are still steps to be taken which will *demonstrate trustworthiness.* Finally, there must be *complete honesty.* This extends to both word and deed. Without these essential ingredients, it is not likely that trust will be effectively reestablished within the marriage.

Creating an Environment for Growth

Many things work together in the creation of an environment or atmosphere that promotes the reestablishment of trust in a marriage. These factors can be viewed as prerequisites for the return of trust. Some of these are set in place by the very process of counseling in which you have already been instrumentally involved. Genuine reconciliation helps the reestablishment of trust and *must* happen. A stated commitment by the offender to the marriage helps and *must* to happen. A determined decision to trust on the part of the betrayed spouse helps and *must* happen. These essential characteristics are historical in nature. They are already present, or at least they should be.

Another counseling-related factor which promotes an atmosphere for trust is not historical. It involves the here-and-now of counseling and even extends well into the future. This prerequisite centers around the willingness of an offender to actually be involved in the ongoing counseling process.

Up to this point in the counseling process, your aim has been to deal with the affair. The goal has been to get *past* the betrayal in order to get *to* the marital relationship. As counseling begins to change its focus—as a couple begins to identify and resolve the historical interferences to marital growth—the willingness of an offender to participate in this process speaks volumes to a formerly betrayed spouse. One encouraged wife phrased it like this:

I see Bill's efforts. He's really trying. I know it's difficult for him, but he continues anyway. That really helps me!

This wife was regaining confidence in her husband. She was witnessing his commitment to the marriage being played out through his continued participation in the counseling process. Trust was being reestablished. The willingness of an offender like Bill to continue in the counseling process not only helps, but it *must* happen. This kind of action helps create the atmosphere for growth. Over time, it can reap immeasurable benefits not only in dealing with marital interferences, but also for the return of trust.

Demonstrating Trustworthiness

Trustworthiness is both a demonstrable and measurable commodity. It involves doing what you say you will do and what is appropriate and legitimate. It is the violation of trust that created the problem in the first place. So when addressing the issue of demonstrating trustworthiness, it would be easy to view it as a problem of appropriateness and predictability. Though these two characteristics are a necessity in all marriages, much less those where there has been betrayal, the type of demonstration that concerns me in betrayed marriages is behavior that indicates a willingness to go the extra mile.

In reestablishing trust, it is sometimes necessary for a spouse to put forth an effort which exceeds normal expectations. In fact, in the eyes of some, this new behavioral expectation may even appear to be excessive. However, desperate situations sometimes require creative solutions. Ben and Carla will help illustrate this principle.

I had met with this couple for several weeks. Restoration was progressing fairly well. After resolving the affair, we had begun to deal with some of the marital issues that had made this marriage particularly vulnerable to betrayal. Ben and Carla each demonstrated a strong commitment to restoring their marriage, and it appeared that we would soon be extending the amount of time between each session. Then we hit a snag. This is how Ben presented it in the session.

Every time I start thinking that things between Carla and me are going pretty well, she does something to make me question that. For instance, she seems to be obsessed with knowing where I am. If I'm supposed to be home by 5:30 and I don't get home until 6:30, she wants to know why. It's like she can't trust me at all. Any deviation from my schedule and she's a wreck.

Something's not right here. This isn't normal. I know lots of men who are occasionally late getting home from work, and they don't get the third degree. What does she expect from me anyway?

I understood Ben's concern, but I also thought his logic was a little faulty. Other men were not getting the third degree, but neither had they betrayed their marriages. Ben probably did not deserve the type of interrogation that he was indicating; however, neither should he expect things to be quite as free as they were earlier in his marriage.

Carla was aware of the problem. She was even a little embarrassed by it. She did not want to complicate their restoration process but felt ambivalent about her behavior. Though part of her felt that her inquiring as to Ben's whereabouts was a demonstration of personal insecurities, another part of her viewed this as appropriate and normal. After all, it was during these unaccountable times that Ben had previously chosen to rendezvous with the other woman. Why shouldn't she be just a little sensitive when he wasn't where he was supposed to be?

I know I appear possessive—even obsessive. I can't help it. I trust Ben. At least, I do most of the time. Even the times when I'm not so trusting are getting shorter and fewer. But I'm not back to the way it was before all of this happened.

I don't know when we'll get back to where it was. I believe I'll get there. It's just going to take me some time. What I need from Ben is a little understanding, acceptance, and as-

sistance. I don't think it's asking too much to know where he's going to be. If something interferes with his plans, I just need to know. I'm not trying to control his life. He doesn't need my permission to go and do; I just need to be kept informed. That's all I need—just a little information and consideration.

Based on the history of their marriage and the point of their recovery from the betrayal, I did not see Carla's expectations of Ben as excessive. If her insecurities persisted for an extended length of time, this would be cause for concern. But for Carla to still have some insecurities regarding Ben's whereabouts at this point in the recovery process was not unusual at all. My concern was whether Ben would be willing to cooperate enough with Carla's short-term needs so as to allow her the time she needed to resolve her fears. In an effort to enlist Ben's cooperation, I used an analogy that I gained from a colleague who dealt with a similar situation.

You know, Ben, this situation between you and Carla is a lot like having a broken leg. There is nothing normal about having a broken leg. It hurts and definitely inhibits your moving around. But what do you do with a broken leg?

(Ben's response) You place it in a cast.

That's right, Ben. That's exactly what you do. You put a cast on the broken leg. Now, is there anything normal about walking around with a cast on your leg? No. Having a cast on is abnormal too.

Do you see where I'm going with this analogy, Ben? Sometimes you move from one abnormal situation to another abnormal situation in order to get back to normal. It's not normal to have a broken leg. Neither is it normal to wear a cast. But you don't put a cast on to be normal—you put a cast on in order to get to be normal later.

The same thing needs to happen in your relationship. Rigidly reporting in to Carla your specific whereabouts is not nec-

essarily normal. Some of what Carla desires would be viewed as excessive in most marriages. But this isn't most marriages; it's your marriage, and there are factors about your marriage that make her needs understandable.

This isn't something that needs to happen forever. Actually, I'd be surprised if it lasted much longer. For the time being, holding yourself accountable for your time would be helpful for Carla personally as it relates to a lessening of her insecurities and for your marriage in general as it relates to the reestablishment of trust. I think your cooperation would demonstrate a trustworthiness that could have far-reaching consequences.

Ben decided to be more cooperative with Carla's expectations. What was good about his decision was that it was not merely an attempt to appease an obsessive woman. Ben recognized the uniqueness of his situation and the short-term rationale for doing what normally would have been considered excessive. As it turned out, Carla did not persist with the insecurities for a long time. Her prediction was accurate; with a little time she was able to more easily release some of the reins. Her being able to let it go was aided by Ben's willingness to go the extra mile.

Complete Honesty

To this point, our discussion has focused on what must be done. It would be easy to also approach the honesty issue from a *do* (as opposed to a *don't*) perspective. However, in assessing the manner in which this issue is usually violated, I believe that greater clarification would come from attending to behavior that must be avoided instead of behavior that must be performed. I intend to point out what honesty *is not*.

A prime example of this form of dishonesty would be found in Randy and his "little white lies." Judy and Randy had been married nearly ten years. During the course of their marriage, Randy had been unfaithful on several occasions. When confronted with the possibility of marital dissolution, Randy chose to turn from his previous life of debauchery, dedicated his life to Christ, and reaffirmed his commitment to Judy and his marriage. Following these decisions, Judy and Randy entered professional counseling.

Judy and Randy had begun counseling with a secular professional but decided to meet with a Christian instead. Much of what they presented at that first session was typical. Judy wanted to know more about the affairs, and Randy wanted to let it lie in the past. What troubled Randy the most was that Judy could not seem to trust him. Again, this was not unusual. What was interesting, though, was Judy's response to Randy's confusion regarding her mistrust. "How do you expect me to trust you when you continue to lie to me?" Judy's statement was fairly indicting. What was Randy's response? He simply smiled and dismissed her concern with the statement: "Judy's only referring to some little white lies that I told. They're not really important." Based on Judy's reaction, it was obvious that she and Randy differed on what was considered important. I suggested they elaborate a little on the situation so I could better understand what was their difficulty.

As a part of Judy's decision to remain in the marriage, she had accepted from Randy a commitment to have no further involvement with any of the women with whom he had previously been unfaithful. While talking at home one evening, Judy casually asked him if he had spoken with any of these other women. She was particularly interested in a woman with whom he had business dealings and would have occasion to see during the course of normal daily operations. Randy had replied, "No." For some reason, Judy had not felt comfortable with this answer. "It could have been paranoia, but I prefer to see it as intuition." At any rate, she pursued this line of inquiry. Finally,

Randy admitted to having a conversation with the woman, but only regarding business.

Randy had lied to Judy. There was no denial of this on his part. Judy's response was one of continued mistrust. What was Randy's defense?

I knew what Judy was really wanting to know. She was really interested in whether I had had any further involvement with this woman. I hadn't. Our contact had been strictly business. But I felt that Judy would not understand this. So I lied.

My motive for lying was good. I wanted to protect Judy from any unnecessary pain. What was the harm in a little white lie?

What was the harm? Not much—unless you value trust in a relationship. Randy was missing the real point. Whether the issue is maintaining trust or rebuilding it, the principle is the same. *There is no right reason for doing the wrong thing.* Randy's goal of protection was at best overprotection prompted by a zeal to spare Judy any form of emotional discomfort. However, I suspect there was at least some degree of self-protection operating in Randy's decision to tell a little white lie. He was not looking forward to Judy's reaction. Regardless of Randy's true motivation, the result was damaging. He would have been far better off to have been honest with Judy, completely honest, even if this honesty caused momentary discomfort for her and possibly him, than to have struck once again at the core of trust.

Cheryl and Larry are another example of the need for complete honesty. Larry had had an affair with a woman at work. The relationship had been maintained with an elaborate plan of deception. I became involved with this couple after the betrayal had been discovered, the illicit relationship severed, and the decision to restore the marriage had been made. Counseling appeared to be productive. However, Cheryl still had concerns about the other woman, knowing that Larry would see her frequently at work.

In order to deal with her own personal discomfort, Cheryl felt that she needed to know if there was any contact between Larry and his former lover. Whether this contact was incidental or otherwise, whether the other woman initiated it or not, and if there was contact, what was said—these were the things that Cheryl needed to hear. Larry was reluctant to provide Cheryl with any of this information. He did not want to upset her. But in a session, Cheryl clearly stated her need for honesty.

(To Larry) I know this is uncomfortable for you, but I need to know. I wonder about it. I won't forever, but for now, this is a concern.

(To Dr. Harvey) I don't want to have to ask Larry if he has spoken to her. I don't want to have to wonder. I want to know that Larry will tell me on his own—that he will initiate the conversation with me when he comes in from work. This will give me some peace. I can let him know when this no longer bothers me.

I trust Larry. I want to trust him more. I just need to know.

Complete honesty. It obviously requires that we do certain things, but it also involves our avoiding others. Little white lies and failing to inform when the need for information has been clearly stated are just two of the easily rationalized activities that can strike at the core of trust. For honesty to contribute toward the reestablishment of trust in a relationship, it must be complete.

Final Thoughts

Part of dealing with the trust issue in a marriage that has been traumatized by adultery is to understand normal processes. In most marriages where couples are grappling with the aftershocks of betrayal, even when everything is being done right, it takes between one and two years for the trust issue to cease being an issue. It's not that there is no change during this period of recovery. Things do get progressively better. But betrayal is a significant blow to a marriage, and it takes a while for trust to return.

It is not unusual for couples to have difficulties in this area, but given adequate time and care, these too should pass. Emphasizing an environment for growth, demonstrated trustworthiness, and complete honesty are three of the means to foster the return of trust, without which a marriage cannot healthily survive.

17

"Why Isn't She Better?"

I had been meeting with Bob and Nancy for several months. The time between sessions had gradually lengthened to the point where as many as two or three weeks would pass before another appointment would be scheduled. This increase in time between sessions was a testimony to their progress. They had long since resolved the issue of betrayal and had been diligently working on their marriage. We had even entered some preliminary discussions of ending our counseling relationship. With this as our background, I found the somber air which placed a pall over today's session to be perplexing.

Neither Bob nor Nancy cared much for facades; they were fairly transparent people. Bob and Nancy were each cordial, quiet, and reserved, but there was a coolness in their interchanges. Little more was volunteered than was required. They did not appear to be angry with one another—only distant. What I *suspected* was that they were discouraged—that after taking the proverbial "three steps forward," something had happened to precipitate the corresponding "two steps backward." As we continued through the session, my suspicion would be confirmed.

Knowing Bob and Nancy as I did, I was certain that they were ready and willing to discuss whatever it was that was troubling them. Neither one of them probably knew exactly how to introduce the subject or who should be the first to bring it up. After some meaningless chatter, I decided it was time to move things along. "Is there something I should know? Things seem to be fairly stilted." It remained quiet for a few moments. Then Bob decided to broach the topic.

I believe we've made a lot of headway in our marriage. Heaven knows we needed to. I guess it just bothers me when something happens that makes me realize that maybe we haven't made as much improvement as I'd like to think. We had an incident last week that brought me back to reality.

To this day, I still don't know what happened. When I left for work that morning everything was fine. We talked a while at breakfast; I kissed Nancy good-bye; and I drove away. But when I got home that evening, something had changed. I didn't notice it at first, but after a while, it seemed that Nancy was in a mood. She seemed quiet and withdrawn. I finally asked if anything was the matter. She said, "No, not really. I just don't feel a hundred percent."

I could tell there was more to it than that. A little later I asked what was really going on. That's when she told me she'd been thinking about the past and it just had her a little bummed out. I didn't know what to say. I still don't. I thought we had gotten past all of that stuff. I guess I was wrong. You know, that has really bothered me. Why is this still a problem? Why isn't she better?

Once again, the office grew quiet. It was Nancy's turn to speak, but she was not yet ready to respond. There was no doubt in my mind that Bob's report was accurate. But Nancy had a look of confusion on her face. Was it regarding what Bob had said? Or was her perplexity more related to not fully understanding her own behavior and emotions?

I can't explain what happened. I wish I could. I'm as confused as Bob and just as disappointed. I think we've made progress—lots of it. But there are times when the memory of what happened just comes flooding back. Some of these flashbacks are predictable—like when we hit certain dates or when we go by places where I know they used to meet. It's the flashbacks that come from unpredictable occurrences that give me the hardest time. I'm least prepared for them.

When the memories return, I experience some pain—not as much as I used to and not for nearly as long a period of time—but I still experience something. I don't want to, but I do. When that happens, I just need a little time to myself and some understanding from Bob. That usually takes care of things pretty quickly. It's when I don't get these that things get bad.

When I see that Bob is bothered by my mood—coupled with the guilt that I'm already placing on myself for not being able to totally get past this—I feel like digging a hole and crawling in it. I just get so discouraged.

The predictables that Nancy talked about are frequently referred to as *anniversary* emotions. They are clearly associated with places and times so as to leave no question as to their impending difficulty. Examples of these would be the time when the affair was discovered or a place the offender and the other woman or man were known to frequent together. The unpredictables, on the other hand, are referred to as *ambush* emotions. The reactions caused by these precipitants are understandable, but the actual culprit is highly idiosyncratic and only recognized after the fact. In Nancy's case, for example, she found herself ambushed by a midafternoon television program in which one of the characters had reportedly had an affair. The fictitious events of the script triggered the recollection of something far from fictitious in Nancy's own life. The memory was unplanned and definitely undesired, but it was triggered nonetheless, and Nancy felt terrible.

Real Questions and Real Answers

"Why isn't she better?" That was Bob's stated question. It sounds legitimate enough. But it's not what Bob was *really* asking. What Bob really wanted to know was *why wasn't Nancy* totally *over the pain of the betrayal.* After all, it had been nearly a year since their reconciliation. He had obviously recommitted himself to both Nancy and their marriage. And he had been doing everything possible to restore their relationship. So what was the problem? Was the pain of the memory ever going to go away? Or was it going to linger on forever?

Answering Bob's stated question would have been simplest. "Why isn't Nancy better?" Simple. *She is better!* Nancy made this clear herself when she described what had been happening regarding the recurrence of the memories of the betrayal.

> When the memories return, I experience some pain—not as much as I used to and not for nearly as long a period of time. But I still experience something.

Nancy was better. The pain was still there, but it had diminished. Months earlier when the betrayal was fresher in her memory, Nancy's pain was excruciating. The depth of the pain and the length of each bout haunted her. However, time and constructive activity on both her and Bob's parts had helped to bring healing to a very deep psychic wound. Time and effort had just not yet brought *complete* healing. Nancy was heal*ing* but not heal*ed.*

Addressing Bob's real question was more difficult. Nancy was not abnormal in her failure to have totally healed from the crisis in her marriage. Betrayal is a significant injury. It is neither quickly nor easily resolved. Healing is a process and usually occurs in layers. As an injured person moves from one plateau to another, things get better with each step that is taken. Distinguishing between a process and something more incidental in nature may provide some clarification here. Whereas a process revolves around the principle of gradations (gradual and incremental changes), incidents are instantaneous. There is nothing instantaneous about healing. An incident may create a wound, but no incident will heal it. Healing will only come as a process—a gradual and time-consuming process.

Bob was caught somewhere in the middle with Nancy—somewhere between comfortably negotiating a process and desiring an instantaneous cure. He had grown *impatient*. Bob began the restoration of their marriage viewing this as a process. He understood that it would take some time, that it would not be instantaneous. But somewhere along the way, he grew weary of the length of the journey. This weariness prompted his discouragement. Though his question spoke to the issue of Nancy getting better, he really wanted to know why she wasn't yet completely over the pain. This underlying question then underwent a transformation. The question actually implied an accusation: "You *should* be over this by now." Though never directly verbalized, this was the message which Bob was beginning to send and which Nancy was beginning to receive. This message was not an accurate assessment of the events, but this perception was beginning to unduly impede the progress of restoration.

Intervention

For Bob and Nancy to have already arrived at this point in the restoration process after weathering so much turmoil suggests that they possess a great deal of strength within their marriage. They may be experiencing an unusually discouraging time, but they are not encountering anything that they cannot face and defeat.

One of the buzzwords for the '90s is the term *empowerment*. Though I'm not one who subscribes to each and every fad or trend in our culture, this term accurately describes my approach in dealing with this lingering artifact of betrayal. I believe couples facing the discouragement precipitated by impatience can be treated as healthy and competent adults—marital partners who are more than capable of hearing and recognizing the truth and then applying it directly to their relationship. Enlightening them with truth then empowers them to solve their own difficulty.

Because of this perspective, my intervention strategy with impatience is basically educational. My first step is to offer *clarification*. This is followed by *education*. The final step, one which the couple will have to accomplish on their own, is *adaptation*. I will continue with Bob and Nancy to illustrate this sequence.

Clarification

Neither Bob nor Nancy was totally aware of the underlying beliefs and attitudes that they were harboring, much less the covert messages that were being communicated. They knew there was discouragement, and they knew it had something to do with a lingering pain from the betrayal. But they had not articulated what they really felt and thought. Sometimes you have to hear your own words from someone else to know what you're really thinking.

Bob needed to know that his disappointment was not with Nancy's failure to improve (for she had), but with her failure to be absolutely healed. This clarification helped bring a redistribution of the problem. Prior to this clarification, the problem was located in Nancy's ineptness. Now there was the added potential of Bob's unreasonableness. Bob was not an unreasonable individual, but his impatience in this matter—his true expectation—was unrealistic. Clarifying what was truly believed and felt, as opposed to what was being stated, offered Bob the opportunity to see just what part of the discouragement he would have to own.

Education

With the clarification of the true attitudes and positions, the foundation was laid for educating Bob and Nancy to what were both legitimate and illegitimate expectations regarding healing. This can be accomplished by describing normal processes in general and also identifying specific instances in the couple's own marriage. For instance, it was *legitimate* to expect that time and constructive effort would result in progress. This would be evidenced by a decrease in both frequency and intensity. These were the very characteristics described by Nancy. It would be *illegitimate* to expect that a wound as significant as betrayal would be totally problem free within a year. It would be nice. It may even be possible in some instances. However, to lift this expectation as a standard which should be reached in all marriages would be illegitimate. Far more reasonable would be an expectation of several years.

There may be some wounds that never totally go away. Years after the restoration process has been completed, some event may occur which unexpectedly prompts a momentary twinge. The brevity of the experience will attest to the healing of the relationship, but the occurrence itself documents that there is still a remembrance. This need not destroy a marriage, nor should it lead to an undue time of discouragement as was represented in Bob and Nancy's relationship. Limited frustration is understandable, but every effort should be made to not offer blame. Identify the situation as the problem and not an individual. The normality of the healing process must be accepted.

Adaptation

Hopefully, clarification and education will compute to an adaptation on the part of the couple. In times of unexpected memory recurrence, the best tactic for couples to follow was illustrated earlier in Nancy's narrative.

When that happens, I just need a little time to myself and some understanding from Bob. That usually takes care of things pretty quickly.

Understanding, as opposed to defensiveness or impatience, is the most constructive response to an unexpected yet lingering pain. Couples who are able to make the adaptation from impatience to acceptance find that healing not only continues, but in all likelihood, will eventually culminate in a complete resolution.

18

Problems for Counselors

The last two chapters have identified attitudinal problems which often inhibit a couple's progress toward restoration. One of the inhibiting attitudes is characteristic of the offended spouse, and the other is characteristic of the offender. It is only fitting to end a book written for counselors with a chapter addressing the attitudinal problems encountered by counselors themselves.

Though it would be the rare counselor who would have difficulties with all of the following problem areas, it would be rarer still to find a counselor who would not wrestle with at least one of these. Whether it be the tendency to prematurely expedite the counseling process, to avoid dealing with the affair altogether, to fail to maintain a clear focus during the counseling relationship, or to settle for less than is essential, any one of these can effectively interfere with the ultimate success of a counselor's intervention.

Too Much Too Soon

Some counselors try to practice the art of counseling at too fast a pace. I notice this mostly with younger, less experienced therapists. There is an urgency about their actions. They seem to operate with a quick-fix mentality as if they were under a mandate to immediately identify and resolve the problem. Though their efforts may have the appearance of being energy and time efficient, there are some things that cannot be rushed.

This variation of performance anxiety can greatly limit the effectiveness of the counseling relationship. Because of the potentially detrimental effects, every effort must be made to defuse the tendency to act prematurely. There are four elements involved in defusing performance anxiety.

Understand the Process

Restoration is a process, not an event. As such, it involves sequential steps and time. There is no miracle cure. There is no way to avoid any of the steps, and there is no way to combine all of the steps into one quick and easy application.

A process is just that—a process. You must allow for gradual transformation. Resist the notion that there is anything you can do to create an instantaneous change. Freeing yourself from that misconception alone can bring a great deal of personal relief.

Know the Steps

Confidence comes from knowing that there is an acceptable plan of action which utilizes the process concept. You know there is the need to first establish a therapeutic relationship. You know there is the need to reconcile a marriage before you can restore it. Being cognizant of what needs to happen (and when) frees you from anxiety-producing confusion.

Figuratively speaking, the winds may be blowing and the sea may be rough, but your ship is not rudderless. Knowing what needs to happen gives you both confidence and calm. You can influence the direction in which the therapy will move.

Plan to Hit Each Step

The restoration process has several steps. You know what they are. Utilizing this knowledge, you can plan to hit each step.

When my office was on the second floor of a building, I used the analogy of climbing stairs to emphasize this concept. Though I knew where my office was located, I did not get there in one giant step. I meticulously hit each step—fifteen of them—in order to reach my destination. Successful counseling involves the same precision.

Be methodical. Utilize clear intent. Patiently *wait* for the appropriate time to intervene. For instance, you know that an offender will need to deal with disclosure, but to deal with this issue in the first session would be inappropriate. Several other steps must precede disclosure. When working with a couple, you know what the couple has successfully accomplished, and you know what is next in their journey. Move them from one step to the next by plan and design.

Remember Your Role

A final element in defusing performance anxiety is the realization of your responsibility. It is not your role to fix this marriage—whether instantaneously or otherwise. You cannot control the actions of others. You may influence their behavior, but ultimately, they are the only ones who can claim responsibility for the outcome of counseling.

Your role is to help them work toward restoration. You will do this to the best of your ability. Maintaining a focus on the present task at hand—on doing the best you know to do—will help keep you from obsessing about, and then jumping to, the ultimate solution.

Avoiding the Affair

A theme of "first things first"—first deal with the affair and then the marriage—has been repeated throughout this book. Still, some counselors prefer to skip the issues related to the actual betrayal—the talking, reconciling, and disclosing—and commence with the marital relationship. Others may give some attention to these issues, but their efforts are of such a token nature that the issues might as well have been avoided altogether.

Why is it that some counselors fail to give the issues of betrayal adequate attention? There are several reasons for this avoidance, but all have their basis in *fear*.

Fear of Intensity

The first fear revolves around personal discomfort. Dealing with the issues of betrayal can prompt emotion-laden sessions. Some counselors find intensity of this magnitude to be extremely stressful. Their solution? Avoid the issues.

This avoidance is self-protective. Though the best interest of the couple may be served by having them deal with the affair, the comfort level of the therapist seems to be the overriding consideration.

Not all counselors experience significant personal discomfort when sessions become intense. For those who do experience some anxiety, not all will allow this to control how they counsel a couple. The issue is not necessarily how a counselor feels but what a counselor does. It is a negligent counselor who allows personal considerations to dictate the flow of treatment.

Problems of this nature are referred to as use-of-self issues. Counselors bring different things into their sessions. Some of what they bring may be good and productive. Some may be not so good and nonproductive. Some of what is brought into a session is recognized whereas some is beyond awareness. Nonproductive tendencies that are not recognized or, when recognized, are allowed to go unchecked, can be problematic for marital restoration. Fear of intensity belongs in this latter grouping.

When in question, assessment of a fear of intensity can be achieved by evaluating your behavior and your feelings. When you know what to do, yet avoid doing it, there is usually a reason. Ask yourself, "What is going on?" Or you may recognize a significant emotional discomfort when intensity rises in sessions. Ask yourself again, "What is going on?" Both of these can be indications that you have a fear of intensity.

Dealing with use-of-self issues can be an ongoing process for a therapist. The following simplified checklist may aid you to assess your own issues and to begin to successfully deal with them:

1. Become aware of your comfort level. Know when you are emotionally uncomfortable.
2. Determine the origin of your discomfort.
3. Begin dealing with this problem by facing and resolving its origin.
4. Recognize the types of counseling situations that trigger your discomfort.
5. Recognize how this discomfort controls your actions as a therapist.
6. Choose to take charge. Do not let the discomfort control your actions.

Fear of Further Hurt to a Spouse

A concern that reviewing what has occurred in the betrayal may create additional yet needless pain for the offended spouse is the underlying presumption with this fear. Failure to deal with the affair due to this concern is actually an example of overprotective behavior.

The goal of any form of counseling is never to bring undue pain, but emotional stress is sometimes unavoidable. In fact, it is frequently a prerequisite to improvement. Regarding betrayal, I find that couples can far better withstand the pain of honesty than they can the nagging and gnawing of the unknown. The known can be grieved. The unknown persists. Though painful, dealing with the affair brings potential for closure and healing. For this reason, overprotection should be avoided.

Fear of Pushing the Offender Away

A concern for how dealing with the affair may affect the offender, and more directly, that it may even change his or her decision to reconcile, is again an example of overprotective behavior. The concept asserts that offenders would feel pushed and badgered if they had to listen to the pain that their betrayal caused. The fear is that some offenders might even decide the marriage wasn't worth this kind of effort. Rather than subjecting them to this experience, especially at a time when the goal is to bring the couple back together and not push them apart, some counselors might completely avoid the issues of the affair.

The possibility that an offender may abdicate when confronted with the pressure of his deeds is just that—a possibility. It could happen, but the consequence of failing to deal with betrayal is far graver. Failing to deal means failing to resolve. Unless the resolution prerequisite is met for the marriage, restoration will be stalled. So what is there to lose? An offender's choice to remain estranged rather than submitting to dealing with the affair is unfortunate, but it is still his choice and his responsibility. Recognize where your boundaries lie.

Failing to Control the Focus

Failing to control the focus of the counseling process is an issue of backsliding. It refers to allowing the attention of the couple to return to the affair after the issues of betrayal have already been appropriately addressed. This is usually a tendency brought on by an obsessive need of the offended spouse. The consequence of this change in focus (reversal) is the complete shutdown of the restoration process. As a counselor, you must guard against any effort to return to the affair once it has been adequately addressed.

When confronted with this problem, it would be good for you to reassess what has already been accomplished in counseling. Work through a checklist.

- Was the affair thoroughly discussed, including the pain of betrayal?
- Were the events of the affair appropriately disclosed?
- Was there a genuine reconciliation including the principal parts: accepting responsibility, expression of remorse, recommitment to the marriage, and changing behavior?

If you question whether any of these areas was adequately handled, it would be good to address it once again. In so doing, however, restate that the goal is to deal with the affair in order to let it go and not to focus on the betrayal for a prolonged period of time. If, on the other hand, you find that the issues surrounding the betrayal have already been adequately dealt with, then it is time for you to take charge of the focus of counseling.

In order to take control, draw attention to what is happening in the session. Reassert the goal of your intervention strategy, what has been attempted thus far, and how they are therapeutically backsliding. You can then formulate some discussion around three themes and sets of questions.

1. Understanding is not legitimization. There is no right reason to do the wrong thing. We know that. We are in no way justifying inappropriate behavior. But understanding does aid us in placing the affair in the past.
2. What is it that you want to see happen regarding your marriage? Is obsessing about the affair going to help you reach this goal? No. Then choose to let it go.
3. What is it going to take for you to let it go?

Creating an atmosphere that brings the covert much more to the surface (overt) will frequently be all that is necessary for the couple to resume the appropriate focus of counseling. If it is not sufficient, then an individual session may be required with the person who continues to obsess. Face it and resolve it so that the focus can be resumed.

Settling for Too Little

Settling for too little generally becomes a problem of the counselor who has difficulty defining an accurate goal in therapy. As a therapist, it is your desire for the relationship to be restored, but restoration is a complex entity. If we view it simplistically, problems can arise. There is a difference between a marriage remaining intact and a marriage becoming reconciled. One requires only the presence of two bodies, whereas the other involves the healing of two spirits. If the focus is only on the retention of the *institution* of marriage, as opposed to both the institution and the *relationship*, then it is easy to settle for too little.

Your goal is for a complete restoration to take place. This necessitates reconciliation. For healing to take place within a relationship, certain things have to happen. As much as you might wish for a couple to stay in a marriage, your desire for them to remain intact should not cloud your vision or interfere with your intervention. Do not end your efforts prematurely or eliminate any necessary elements. You need to do what is required to bring restoration and not merely settle for a couple staying together. Without true restoration, their staying together will likely be only time limited. Your goal is health—not merely appearance.

Final Thoughts

Though the content of *Surviving Betrayal* has dealt with infidelity and marital restoration, the focus has been upon practicing the art of therapy. The structure presented has stressed the theme that you must first deal with the affair before you can proceed to the more important work of restoring the marriage.

The steps required in accomplishing this transition—resolving the affair, bringing a couple to the point of reconciliation, confronting the blocks to restoration, and successfully moving the focus from the incident of the affair to the marriage as a relationship—have been thoroughly articulated. But I would be remiss if I failed to acknowledge that there is more to counseling than merely practicing an art.

We need to strive to do the best we can. This involves being conscientious—recognizing what aids and what hinders the counseling process. But we cannot lose sight of the fact that an essential ingredient to any form of counseling is genuinely caring for the person you are counseling. *Why* are you doing *what* you are doing?

There are all kinds of reasons for practicing the art, but unless you care, your intervention will likely be in vain. Be circumspect. Reach out to your clients and be sure that you are extending to them what Jesus has already extended to you.